FAITH OF A
MUSTARD SEED

PAUL KARANICK

authorHOUSE®

AuthorHouse™
1663 Liberty Drive
Bloomington, IN 47403
www.authorhouse.com
Phone: 1-800-839-8640

Edited by M'chel Martinez and Christina Karanick

Published by AuthorHouse   05/15/2012

ISBN: 978-1-4772-0347-7 (sc)
ISBN: 978-1-4772-0345-3 (hc)
ISBN: 978-1-4772-0346-0 (e)

Library of Congress Control Number: 2012908514

Any people depicted in stock imagery provided by Thinkstock are models, and such images are being used for illustrative purposes only.
Certain stock imagery © Thinkstock.

To my wife and children (Christina, Grace, Hannah and Nathan) who have endeavored together with me in the calling God has placed on our lives. To my parents, Billy and Betty Karanick, who have raised me to have faith in Christ. To Chaze and Brianna Karanick and the Xclaimed Ministries Band for using their amazing talents to serve God.

Foreword

Sometimes being effective requires us to change. It is quite obvious that Pastors Paul and Christina Karanick understood this truth when they formed Xclaimed Ministries. Their keen perception into the needs of the unchurched people of their area, and the leadership of the Holy Spirit, motivated them to pursue different methods of community outreach.

The Karanick's loving analysis of these needy people, who were unreached by any church, convinced them that this segment of the population were not likely to go to any church; so Paul and Christina Karanick took *church* to the people. They found real *hurts to heal*. They found real *needs to meet*. Both the *context* and the *content* were different than *normal* church.

Outdoor concerts, free food provided, free toys for children, drawings for free bicycles for children, free Bibles, New Testaments and Gospels of John are key components. A consistent highlight and focus is the interesting and inspirational Gospel message from Paul Karanick, that is always concluded with a respectful, motivating invitation for people to come forward for prayer to receive Jesus Christ as Savior.

I have been among the teary-eyed participants at these Xclaimed events, who observed the unquestionable working of the Holy Spirit applying the Bible truth to needy hearts, and drawing them to the Savior! I have stood among the crowd during Paul's invitation at the end of his message, and quietly praised and thanked God for the overwhelming spiritual fruit that resulted.

It is so amazing to realize that each of these Xclaimed events are provided by faith regarding the financial expense. Courage, risk, faith, obedience, zeal and commitment are among the terms that describe this creative Ministry. As you read *Faith of a Mustard Seed* you will hear Paul Karanick's heart. I trust that his and Christina's example of faith will be an inspiration for you as it has been for me.

Norman Moore, Evangelist
Long Beach, California

Preface

In the body of Christ, we all have gifts of the Spirit. One of mine is faith; however, for most of my life, it was just a small amount of faith. As I grew in my relationship with God, I discovered that He not only provides us with gifts but God builds a relationship with us as He enables us to use the gifts He provides.

I realized that a spiritual relationship with God is similar to physical relationships with our own loving family. Something as simple as a dad playing catch with his children creates a greater bond between them. The children may already have gifts of throwing and catching the ball, but each time they throw and catch the ball they increase their abilities.

Each of us have gifts. As we increase our time and relationship with God we are able to increase our abilities and understanding of these gifts and can use them more effectively for God's work. *Faith of a Mustard Seed* is a testimony of how God worked in our lives as a ministry written with the hope that others will grow in their walk with God as well.

Introduction

Faith can be elusive. Where it begins and how far it can stretch one as a person becomes a moving target. But, faith is essential to the quality of our relationship with Jesus Christ. I am predisposed to study the concept, but education can only take one so far. Faith should produce action and when the Lord revealed His plan for us; action was the only appropriate reaction.

When the Lord calls you to do something for Him, make action your reaction. Take what you have learned from your days of Bible Study and put your faith into motion. A story of great faith is inspiring and, when shared, can move others to action.

It is for that reason, to inspire others, that I am overjoyed that my husband took the time to record this walk of faith in a book. This is **our story of action** and on many occasions I still pinch myself to see if it is real. God has led us from the beginning; from how we met, to our miracle children and to an exciting ministry. But, it is also important to reveal how the Lord grew our faith in the midst of our shaky beginnings, our starts and stops and our times of fear.

The entire story stands as a testimony to what God can do with people who have a small amount of faith and who make action their reaction.

Christina Karanick

The Grande Finale

On July 7, 2007, the gates at the Rose Bowl Stadium in Pasadena, California opened for a free evangelistic concert. Over 9,000 people gathered to hear music from Skillet, Leeland, The Afters, KJ-52, Warren Barfield, Decyfer Down and worship by the Xclaimed Ministries Band. After years of praying, planning and waiting it finally all came together. After Leeland performed their last song, it was time for me to take the stage.

God had called me several years ago to begin this outreach and now it was time to deliver the Good News of Jesus Christ. The amusing thing about God calling *me* is that I have never preached to such a large crowd. Until now, the largest crowd to which I have ever preached was 400 people. I stepped onto the stage and began to speak. I quickly realized that no one could hear me because my headset microphone did not work. Not part of the plan! The stage manager handed me a hand held microphone and I continued to speak. As a very animated preacher, having to hold a microphone was a bit of a handicap. I can't recall ever holding a microphone in past events. I suppose there is no better time to get out of your comfort zone than in front of 9,000 people. As I am doing a personal introduction for the audience, the stage helpers are setting up the screen that displays my sermon notes. After they were completely off the stage I realized that the screen was working but my notes were not there. No one, besides me, can see the screen is blank. Here I stand before 9,000 people with a handheld microphone and no notes.

Amazingly Relaxed

Through the last few years of putting this event together, my faith in God has strengthened tremendously. As I was standing on that stage, even with the technical issues, I had so much comfort knowing God was in control. I can truly say God had prepared me for such a time as this. I spoke on how God has a plan for each of us and how Satan will try to steal that plan away by enticing us with other things. The Scripture was from Genesis regarding Adam and Eve. God had given them everything. They had the perfect life. They only had one commandment which was to not eat off of one tree; everything else was fine. However, Satan steps in with lies and convinces them that they can be like God if they eat from that one tree. Once they disobeyed God by eating the fruit of that tree, they forfeited God's original plan (the perfect plan) and opened the door for sin, corruption and death.

God has a plan for each of us and it is an amazing and wonderful plan. Don't allow Satan to steal it from you! Seek God's will in your life and do it; don't settle for anything that Satan has to offer.

At the end of the sermon, I gave an opportunity for people who would like to accept Jesus into their lives to come down to the field so that our counselors could pray with them. We had hundreds of pastors waiting on the field to pray with anyone who responded to the call. This was my first large event and I wasn't sure what to expect. I looked up to the thousands of people in the stands and it seemed that not even one person was moving.

The two learning highlights of my journey over the previous few years were: To **trust** in Him and to **wait** on Him. He is always in control!

Be Patient and Wait

I knelt down on the stage and I began to pray a silent prayer—one on one with God. I couldn't believe that I had sold our apartment, spent all of our money and put my family through two years of trials and tribulations to not even have one person come to accept Christ in their life. After that moment with God, I looked up and to my surprise hundreds of people had responded and come down to the field. It's like God was reconfirming to be patient and wait. I had just learned one powerful lesson in mass evangelism; it takes <u>time</u> for people to come down to the field! I did not realize the amount of time it took for people to get out of their seats and make it down to the field. Over 500 came down to the field and we had at least 265 commitments to Christ. We know that there could have been many more that accepted Christ, but we only counted the ones who acknowledged it to one of the pastors or completed an information card. We did not want to assume someone merely coming down to the field meant that they would ask Christ into their life. Each pastor on the field had the responsibility to pray with the individuals in their small group, get basic contact information, then help each person get connected to a Christian Bible-teaching church. The pastors played a very important role in the success of these new believers. It is an awesome experience to become a new Christian and accept Jesus into your life; however, without being discipled and encouraged by mature Christian brothers and sisters it is too easy to lose that new found life.

BarlowGirl was unable to make it to the event. Their airplane had mechanical trouble and they never left the airport.

Now for the final event of the night, I went into the audience to watch the band Skillet bring this night to a close. As I was waiting for the band to take the stage, I was approached by a church youth group that came from Arizona to attend this event. They introduced me to several who had rededicated their life to Christ and a teenage girl who had accepted Christ for the first time. A father sitting nearby introduced me to his son (about eight years old) and said he wanted me to know that he had accepted Jesus into his life at the invitation.

As I walked outside the stadium, many people stopped me to share stories of how the Holy Spirit had touched them through the Lord's Message. After putting so much of our lives into this event, it was encouraging to hear the confessions of faith. I would have done it for ONE saved soul, but the blessing that I received by witnessing so many changed lives made my heart leap!

It is very interesting how God works in our lives. When God called me to begin this ministry I thought I was going to put on an evangelistic concert to reach the lost. God, however, had much more in mind. During the few years of planning and preparing for this event, God broke me down and rebuilt all that I understood about faith. God took this occasion and strengthened my relationship with Him. Now, I could see that in God's eyes it wasn't all about the event; it was also about our relationship and teaching me how to have faith in Him completely.

Will the Small Church Please Stand Up?

I grew up as a preacher's kid. For many years I could not figure out why our churches never seemed to have many people in them. **I always asked myself, "Why doesn't anyone do anything to get more youth** in the church?" Our church youth group normally consisted of me, my brother and one, maybe two of our friends. I remember attending Avondale Elementary School in Birmingham, Alabama. My friends that attended other churches seemed to always be involved in something with their churches and they always seemed to have lots of youth in their churches. I can remember standing at the windows in the classroom talking to my friends about what we did over the weekend. They seemed to always be doing something fun with their church youth group. Things like camping, biking, concerts and other remarkable activities. I spent time at church but my weekend was nothing like their experience. I went to church Sunday morning with about 30 people (total) and later that night with even less people. The church had some activities but very few people would show up.

God, You Want Me To Do What? Seriously?

Many years later, I was living in California. I was married and had one daughter, when the familiar question flashed through my mind. **"Why doesn't anyone do anything to get more youth in the church?"** I then directed the same question to the Lord. As I was driving past the Anaheim Convention Center, I realized that the question needed be changed from "Why doesn't anyone do anything to get more youth in the church?" to **"What am I going to do to get more youth in the church?"** As I passed by, I impulsively picked up the cell phone and called the Anaheim Convention Center to ask how much it would cost to rent out the arena for one day. The representative would not give me an exact amount but she said the base began at $7,500 with the addition of the cost of employees, parking, security, etc. I asked her if she thought the whole day could cost less than $50,000 and she cautiously said it could be done.

I was so excited by this news that I hurried home and walked into my house and looked at my wife and said, "You know our four unit apartment building in Dana Point? I want to sell it and pay for a one day Christian concert at the Anaheim Convention Center. It will cost about $50,000." I explained how God had been putting this on my heart for many years but I did not realize that he was calling *me* to do this until today.

What Did You Do With My Wife?

Now, my wife is a financially risk-free person. I am the visionary and risk taker; she is my polar opposite. I have big ideas and, she being the realist is always quick to find the logical reason it will not work. For example, I could say, "I have a great idea; we should create a soda that has no caffeine, with a citrus flavor." She will calmly look at me and ask, "Have you ever heard of 7UP or Sprite?"

I am a visionary and she is detailed oriented. She grounds me and works out how my visions can come to life.

When I came home with this grand idea to sell the apartment building (which was supposed to be saved for either our retirement or our children's education), she amazingly agreed with me. Not accepting the answer so easily, I restated it to her; "I said that we should sell the apartment building—our retirement plan—to pay for a one day, evangelistic Christian concert." She agreed once again and stated that we should do whatever God has put on my heart. That scared me more than anything because something seemed wrong about her quick approval. She is the person that pulls me back down to reality. This time she began to float in the clouds with me. I did not know if I should be excited or fearful because of her response!

At this time in my life, I was the Associate Pastor at the Stanton Lighthouse Community Church of the Nazarene and I was also the website designer for the Anaheim District Church of the Nazarene. Now that my wife gave me the OK, I just needed to run it by Dr. Ray Doane, our denomination's District Superintendent to see what he thought. I entered into his office and threw this idea at him and he, without hesitation says, "Sure let's go do it." I take a deep breath and ask him, "You do realize that I am just your computer guy and that I really have no clue what I am doing?" He encouraged me to do what God had put on my heart and he supported what I planned to do. Now, I am really afraid. This seems a bit too easy for such a huge notion. I seriously thought that either my wife or Dr. Doane would have brought me back to earth, but I suppose God talked to them before I arrived.

What's in the Name

One of my first tasks was to come up with a name for this event and ministry. I started out in the morning driving and trying to think of a name. I truly wanted to use the letter X which in Greek symbolizes Christ. All day I had blurted out names but nothing seemed to be what I was looking for. I had read every sign and billboard along the highways to see if anything sounded right. At about 9:30 pm I was about 2 miles from my home and I prayed and asked God, "Why can't you just help me with a name?" I had spent a full day trying to come up with a name and my mind was blank. I thought this would be fairly easy since I knew the concept I was trying to accomplish. After praying and being a bit frustrated with my inability to come up with a simple name and knowing I was close to being home for the day; I stopped at a traffic light and it seemed to be taking a while but as I was continuing to pray I looked out my right window and these big red letters on a restaurant stood out to me "Claim Jumper". I started saying X jumper, X jump, Christ jump, Christ Jumper, Xclaim, Christ claim and that sounded good. So I continued to work with that, "Christ claim" or "Christ claimed." Then finally that was it, "Christ claimed." In those last two miles God had revealed the name.

"X" comes from the Greek letter Chi, which is the first letter of the Greek word Χριστός, translated as "Christ".

x•claimed: [ik-skleym /d]
1. Christ claimed
2. claimed by Christ through the cross
3. Christ has paid the price and redeemed all those who believe in Him.

I walked into the house told my wife I had the name Xclaimed—meaning Christ claimed—and the next words out of her mouth confirmed that it was the name, "Get on the web and see if you can get the domain name." I purchased every version of that name that I could think of.

Now I have had some wild ideas in my life but never anything like this. Not long after we began, I felt so convinced about this name and ministry that I went to trademark the name. I have never done that in my life. But I felt compelled to do it. I went online and started the trademark process. I believe that God calls us to do His work; however, I also believe He has a backup plan if we say "No." I found out about two weeks after submitting the trademark. A very large Christian psychologist ministry called me and stated that they too were attempting to trademark the name and had seen that I was also in the process of trademarking the name. It was amazing that God had given me the insight to trademark the name but it also confirmed that if I had I told God "No" or "wait a while"—He had someone else prepared to go ahead and do His work.

I had begun requesting information from the Anaheim Convention Center about what was necessary to put a concert together but I needed to come up with a date. My brother, Chaze, had mentioned in casual conversation that in the upcoming year on June 6, 2006 the date would be 666. At that time it did not mean much beyond being a very interesting thought. In the next week or so all the district pastors had a day at the Anaheim Angels baseball game. I was given a seat about 3 or 4 seats from Dr. Doane. After I had sat for a little while I realized that I had not put my credit card back into my wallet. I took a glance at it and realized that the expiration date was July 2007. I remembered what my brother had said about June 6, 2006 and realized that July 7, 2007 would be 777. I looked at Dr. Doane and shouted to him, "I know the date for the event; July 7, 2007 and it is on a Saturday which is the 7th day of the week". So, we have the seventh day of the seventh month of the seventh year on the seventh day of the week. God's Word does not specifically say that God's favorite number is seven but we know that He uses it in reference to some really good things and as a number for completion. It was amazing how God was helping me put this together. He has to make it very simple for people like me.

Another thing I noticed that was across from the Angel Stadium was the Arrowhead Pond of Anaheim. I told Dr. Doane that the Pond would be a cool place to have the event. The next week I contacted the Convention Center and they could not reserve the 777 date because it was too far in advance, they will only go out one year. I remembered seeing the Arrowhead Pond and called them. They reserved the date for us and we were well on our way. The bad news was that the cost was now around $80,000, but we had equity in our apartment building and I was prepared to use it.

"Walk by Faith not by sight." *(2 Corinthians 5:7, NASB)*

It did not take long at all for me to realize that I had no clue what I was doing. However, I was certain that God had called me for this ministry and He would faithfully supply everything that I needed to accomplish what He has started.

'And I am sure of this, that He who began a good work in you will bring it to completion at the day of Jesus Christ.' *(Philippians 1:6, NASB)*

God calls us to do astonishing works in His name; many times it requires gifts, talents and abilities that are beyond our means. Philippians 1:6 not only confirms that God is working within us spiritually, but it also confirms that God is working with us physically and He will not leave us stranded without the resources we need. God provides and He provides on time. We often want God to provide on our command as in the fairytale stories of a magic genie. Well, God is not a genie and he knows what we need and when we need it. He looks for us to cast our cares upon Him and allow Him to lead us step by step.

Life Verse

A group of pastors asked me recently, what is a Scripture that has significantly affected my life? Feeling very confident in my answer, I responded, "2 Corinthians 5:7 *'Walk by faith not by sight'*." They all chuckled at the response and one replied, "Well, at least it wasn't the shortest verse in the Bible, 'Jesus wept'." As the months progress in this journey that God has called me and my family to endure, these six words of 2 Corinthians 5:7 would become one of our greatest sources of knowledge and hope. We learned to exist by these words. There were many times we did not know how we would be able to get finances, resources, volunteers, a venue, and many other necessities, but we continually relied upon this Scripture to lead and encourage us. We could not always see what or how God was going to provide; we simply had to have faith that He would provide. It became such a part of our lives that we used it on all our Xclaimed T-shirts, emails, and website. God does not always provide a list of steps that we can carry with us to reach the goal. He usually leads us and expects us to seek the answers as we go. This builds a greater relationship with Him and it keeps us in a place of depending upon His strength and knowledge. If He were to give us a list of steps to perform to reach our objective, we may find it a little tempting to do it alone without God. Once we leave God out, we miss the relationship that He was intending to come out of the calling. God wants to be involved with our lives, not to be a bystander. He loves us and wants to reveal Himself personally to us as we walk in His ways.

Let the Trials Begin

There came a time that I was given the opportunity to speak to a group of pastors from the Anaheim area to explain my vision. In a room of about 40 pastors, I began to tell my story of how God had called me to have an evangelistic event. Once I gave all the details there was a voice from the room that stood in opposition to this idea. He was a pastor of a local church. He is known in the area for starting up discipleship and church growth programs, so this opposition surprised me. Nonetheless, his statement grabbed the attention of the room and put doubt in the minds of the pastors. One of the comments that stood out the most was that he did not see why I would be doing a big event since, in his opinion; they aren't successful in the long term. He stated that people need to be discipled and he did not feel that mass evangelism was the way to go. The other pastors lost the little enthusiasm that they may have had after a negative statement like that was raised. The idea was now tainted with doubt.

His opinion had merit but I think that we need to first reach the lost. Let's reach the lost, lead them to Jesus as their Lord and Savior and then, I agree, let's focus on making disciples. It is sad to say that church is sometimes its own worst enemy. I did eventually come to realize that my biggest giants to face were not money or event production; opposition would come from within the church, specifically those people who have always done "church" the same way. It really disappoints me when people continue to do the same thing year after year even though it continues to fail. I strongly believe that Jesus expects us to reach as many people with the Gospel of Christ by all means possible. Let's reach the lost with evangelism and teach them with discipleship. Jesus Himself, did both. He taught to the masses and He also discipled His followers. Many times we stand in our own way of doing God's work. From a pastor's point of view, this pastor should have remembered how Jesus preached to the masses on several occasions and how Peter did the same with thousands being converted to Christ (Acts 2:41). God reminds me through His word that it was within His ministry that He also faced this same type of opposition. When Jesus was speaking to His disciples and telling the things that must happen for God's plan to be fulfilled Peter stood up and basically claimed that he did not approve of that plan but he had one that would work better.

Jesus turned and said to Peter, **"Get behind me, Satan! You are a stumbling block to me; you do not have in mind the things of God, but the things of men."** *(Matthew 16:23, NASB)*

Jesus was not literally calling Peter Satan; in its original meaning he is calling him an adversary. Peter, although he thought he was doing a good thing, was actually hindering the work of God. The pastor that voiced his opinion probably meant to speak the right thing, but he actually caused others and himself to be blinded to the actual work that God was calling in my life. Sometimes we become so involved in the ministry that we actually stop looking at the direction God is leading us towards. We are to reach the lost and Satan would love to blind the church to this calling. When we get to the point that we feel that spreading the Word of God to the world is not an effective way to lead people to Christ we should stop and question if that thought would be coming from God. The Bible says that Satan is a liar. When we listen to him we will be deceived. There are many times he will tell us that we are right but if we look at God's plan we can see how wrong we are in God's eyes. Satan does not want us to reach the lost; therefore, he will try to convince us that what we are doing is not correct. This is why it is so important to know God's Word and to be certain through confirmation that God has called us for a specific task. When we are sure of doing God's will then Satan cannot easily get us off track. Had I not known what God put on my heart was true, then I would have easily believed other people's opinions. Job faced this with his three friends. They continued to give him advice yet it was not from God. God later rebukes them for speaking mistakenly (see Book of Job).

Wounded not Defeated

The battle we fight when following Christ is so real and anyone doing God's work can feel the spiritual battles that take place. It wasn't long before Satan would try to derail our ministry once again. Over the next few months, my wife and I formed a team of volunteers to help me with this vision. This was one of my greatest learning experiences. I have always thought that I knew who I was as a person, but I had a lot to learn about myself and God took the time to teach me how to grow in Him. One of the hardest self-realizing factors that came about was learning that I am not a good "idea" communicator. I am a visionary and not a detailed one. I see the BIG picture and the end result. What that means is that I confuse a lot of people. During our first meetings it wasn't so bad because people wanted to hear the BIG picture idea. The issues began when people wanted more defining answers. They began to ask me questions like, "You want to have this event on July 7, 2007; will that conflict with 'Greg Laurie's Harvest Crusade?", "How will we advertise the event?", "Who are the bands?", "Where will we get all the volunteers to help at the event?" The list of questions continued to grow and unfortunately, I did not have any answers. God put on my heart to do this but he hadn't given me any thoughts on how I would actually put it all together. Remember, this is all out of my abilities and

I have never put anything together like this in my life. These were great questions that I simply did not have the ability to answer.

I learned quickly that I was a visionary who needed someone with details capability. God knows me best and in 2003 (years earlier), He had me marry my wife who I came to realize was more and more a part of His BIG plan. Christina is extremely detailed. As the meetings continued and I would freak everybody out with the BIG picture view, "The event that we are working on now is great but eventually, I want to have a concert every two months!" This is where I lose my committee and where Christina would bring the meeting back into perspective by saying simple phrases like, "What Paul is talking about is in the future and the final outcome. Let's look at the first steps in obtaining that goal." When God calls you to do His work, He knows your weaknesses and be assured that He has already made preparations for them to be handled.

Another one of my faults is that I am a fanatic about faith. It is not a fault in the sight of God, but it drives people crazy! People are comfortable when they see a plan and the finances to accomplish that plan. I am comfortable when I have those items also. However, when God calls, he doesn't always give the plan nor reveal the financing. My calling is to have faith that the *One who has started a good work in me will complete it.*

Even though I have faith, I will soon find that I only have a little faith compared to what I truly need in my life.

Show Me the Money

As months went by, people would discuss more and more about the finances. As I had planned, we listed our property in Dana Point for sale. The unplanned part was—it wasn't selling! We have been planning for months for this event and the financing to come from the proceeds of the sale. God opened my eyes to the fact that the building was not going to be as easy to sell as I had hoped. The pressure came quickly from the committee to find answers for funds. As the trials got harder my faith grew stronger. I would tell the committee to have faith. God is not only calling us to simply do this event, He is calling us to have faith. He will provide what we need in His perfect timing. I have always been disappointed in the way many churches handle a crisis. It seems that when a church goes through a hard time they complain and beg the congregation for money or whine about the disaster that they are facing and how the end of their ministry may be imminent. I feel the church needs to use these times to strengthen what we believe about our faith in Jesus Christ. If we believe that God is all powerful, all knowing, and will never leave us nor forsake us; then let's act accordingly. The church should bring the congregation to the knowledge of the crisis, but as Paul and Silas did when they were going through persecution being beaten and thrown into prison, let's praise God, rejoice and worship Him whom we trust and believe.

"But about midnight Paul and Silas were praying and singing hymns of praise to God, and the prisoners were listening to them; and suddenly there came a great earthquake, so that the foundations of the prison house were shaken; and immediately all the doors were opened and everyone's chains were unfastened." (Acts 16:25-26, NASB)

He is very capable of supplying our needs and He is willing and ready to do just that in our lives. As the church rejoices during trials, the people will see the example to apply in their own lives. We often make decisions based upon our fear. It is as if fear is leading us. God wants us to be led by Him through faith. I have found that it is better to pursue a life led by faith rather than fear; hope rather than doubt. Too many times we allow fear to direct our lives and allow doubt to drown our hope. Through faith we should seek the direction of the Holy Spirit.

Let's Try This Again

Opportunity seemed to be knocking at my door when Dr. Ray Doane, the District Superintendent for the Anaheim District Church of the Nazarene, asked me to re-address the pastors at a pastor and wife's retreat in Laguna Hills, California. By now, I had a better description of the event and was a little more polished in my presentation. The General Superintendent from Kansas City was also at this event and was the main speaker for the weekend. I stood up in front of the audience and told them how I felt that God put a calling on my heart to evangelize with an event-based outreach; a free concert with local bands and evangelistic message. I also updated the information for the ones that had heard me announce this event at the other meeting. For one, the location changed. I wanted to use the date of July 7, 2007 due to it being a Saturday and its date being 7-7-7. How cool is that? The Anaheim Convention Center was already booked for that day so we looked for another venue (because of the date issue and some other restrictions). I called the Arrowhead Pond of Anaheim and for $80,000 I could have our event there. It scares me now, that this did not scare me at that point. I literally did the math in my head; the event at the convention center would have been about $50,000, so we go up

$30,000 then add some miscellaneous costs for the event—let's say $20,000. We are now at $100,000. We still have enough equity in the apartment building to pay for the event and have money for savings. So, with that logic and faith we reserved the Pond. After giving more detail and showing how we can reach thousands of people I returned to my seat and the service resumed. Not five minutes later, one of the pastors called me outside. "I love what you were saying. We need something like this. So who are the bands going to be? I have a few ideas of some I know. Who is the speaker? How about Franklin Graham? Have you contacted him?" As he was speaking, another pastor walked up and asked, "Who will be the speaker that day? I have a few people I think would be awesome." I did not plan on this being my first questions and I guess I wasn't as prepared as I should have been. I replied, "I feel like God is calling me to be the speaker. We will have some local bands and I will give an evangelistic message." Obviously, that wasn't the correct answer for them. They both said, "Oh, OK." then, returned to the meeting. Another pastor stepped up and said, "I like what you were saying, but how can this help my church? I would love to get involved if I can find a way that it would help us."

It didn't take too many more conversations before I was feeling pretty down about this whole thing. I now feel silly that I don't have any bands picked out, the speaker isn't anyone well known (or known at all), and I did not realize that some churches will not participate if it is a Kingdom building event and not a local church building event. I made my way back into the meeting and but could not listen. I was so disheartened that I really was about to cry (Yes, I am a guy and I really was about to cry!). Instead, I opened my Bible and began to read. I opened to Ezekiel 13. I don't think I have ever read Ezekiel, but I looked down and these are not the exact words but this is how I read it as being from God, *I did not call you—you are not doing my will. Stop telling everyone that this is from me. I did not give this to you.* It was painful to read and as if I had been yelled at by God.

"Therefore, thus says the Lord GOD, "Because you have spoken falsehood and seen a lie, therefore behold, I am against you," declares the Lord GOD." (Ezekiel 13:8, NASB)

Now, I have had it! Not only did the people have a different opinion than what I was looking for, but God Himself is slapping me with His rebuking. I could not take it any longer; I left the meeting and went up to my hotel room. I literally closed the door and screamed at God (respectfully as I could be at this point—I still understand that He is God). "How could you do this to me? Out of your own Word, you claim that if we have the faith of a mustard seed we could move mountains. "I have had faith enough to put my property up for sale, convince my wife to go along with this crazy idea, form a committee of people who want to be part of this ministry, stand before pastors and other leaders and proclaim what you have told me to do and then after I do all this you are going to tell me that you did not tell me to do this? To stop telling people that you said these things? Why couldn't you have told me many months ago? Why wait until I announce it to hundreds of people?"

After allowing me to vent my frustrations God made it real clear to me as he put on my heart, "Open your Bible." I replied, "What?" "Open your Bible and re-read that same chapter in Ezekiel; except this time do not start in the middle! Start from the beginning of the chapter." I began to read it again and found it was amazingly encouraging. God was not telling me to stop. In this chapter, He was telling His Prophet what to tell the people that were out prophesying, but God had not called them to prophecy. In my case, God saw that people were coming up out of the crowd and giving me their vision or thoughts on how they would like to see this event structured. God was coming to my rescue (Had I read it from the beginning I would have seen that). He was simply saying that He had given me this vision. He had not given it to the others—this was what He called me to do; they each have their own calling. God gave me His Word to listen to Him only; others need to stop telling me what they would like to have happen and realize that God has already spoken and He is leading me where He wants me to take this event. God may give them vision, but not for this event and He was making that clear. Yes, I had to apologize to God again. I don't know when I will ever understand that He is always in control, He wants the best for us and He is never wrong. It is important to be confident in God's calling. If we are not sure of what God has asked us to do, then we will be easily swayed by others suggestions and opinions. Keep focused on God and His will. It is another step in growing in faith as God encourages us along the way.

Faith Without Works is Dead

After the meeting, I walked up to one of the church leaders and asked what he thought of the event we were planning. He gave the typical response "That takes a lot of faith, we will be praying for you and your event." Maybe I am naive or something, but I think if he really meant that he would have said something to the effect of "Can we help you finance this event? Let's meet at another time and see how the church can assist you. Let's publish this on our news broadcast." In the Book of James, the writer mentions that if a person comes to you hungry and naked do not simply bid him farewell, but do the actions to accomplish it (the work that backs up your words). At some point the church needs to step up instead of away. We need to have the hands on approach instead of hands off. Imagine how much more we could accomplish if the entire body of Christ (the church) actually functioned as one body.

"What use is it, my brethren, if someone says he has faith but he has no works? Can that faith save him? If a brother or sister is without clothing and in need of daily food, and one of you says to them, "Go in peace, be warmed and be filled," and yet you do not give them what is necessary for their body, what use is that? Even so faith, if it has no works, is dead, being by itself." (James 2:14-17, NASB)

I feel it is time for the church to stop talking about what Jesus can do in people's lives and start showing that it is real. We need to be examples. People are looking for the genuine Christians. They are looking for our words to be verified through our works. If we believe Jesus is God and prayer changes everything; why do we worry so much? Why aren't we praying more often and expecting God to perform on our behalf? As I mentioned earlier, it is extremely important to confirm that God has called you before acting upon an idea or calling. Satan will try everything he can to get you off course. You must be sure in knowing your goal and knowing that God is with you during it all.

Moving Ahead During the Unknown

It did not take many more committee meetings before a suggestion was made that we get a professional production company to produce this event. The production company could take what we envisioned and make it happen. We contacted a local production company in Orange County, California. They handle most of the Christian events in that area. A few of us from the committee met with them and it seemed flawless. They liked our event and they would give us an estimate shortly. About one week later, we met again to go over the cost breakdown. They replaced the local bands with headliner bands so that we could get a draw of people close to 13,000. Now with this new list of bands, production costs, etc., we are now looking at a cost of about $285,000. The event sounded awesome. I was looking for a festival style event with one stage, shopping, and car show outside and one stage inside for the main presentation. I am not sure where faith turns into stupidity, but I know God is able to do all things. The cost had increased significantly, but we still had equity in the property, so if the property sold for the asking price we could pay for this or at least close enough to raise the rest. So, we agree to go with the plan and put up the deposits once the property sells.

Getting the Word Out

Dr. Doane began to call me to preach at several of the churches in his district. He is the one person that I can say truly had faith in what we were doing and completely backed us up in our endeavor. He continued to try to get us recognized and financed. In the long haul, he ends up helping us beyond his means even putting his own money in for support. As I began to preach at these churches, I found that a few people would not like my style of preaching. For example, when I illustrate that Goliath is 9.9-10.9 feet tall I stand up on a stack of soda crates to show how tall that is; I am short, so it take plenty of crates. One church called me back a second time, the pastor mentioned that they needed me to fill in for another Sunday, but a few people said if I bring the soda crates back they won't stay for the service. I responded to the pastor, "They do realize that I don't use the crates for every sermon; right?" On another occasion, another church sent me way back in time. As I approached the building I noticed a church member sitting at the front door. As I began to enter, the man at the door stopped me and said, "Do you need a comb for your hair?" I thought he was kidding. Nope, he was extremely serious. My hair is a semi-spike. He said, "If your hair is like that I won't stay for the sermon". A few months later, I was asked to come and preach again—and sure enough, the next time I preached there the same man met me at the door once again and this time asked me if I was going to go get dressed before I preach! He wanted me to go get my suit! I always wonder what these types of Christians would have done about John the Baptist or even Jesus Himself.

Confidence through Trials

For the most part, our ministry gained momentum. Aside from a few issues, it seemed that people of all ages liked our ministry and what we were accomplishing. My brother, Chaze Karanick, put together a band and we began to outreach by creating a service called "Revive!" We tried our best to make it a service that the entire family would enjoy attending. Our first "Revive!" service was at a church in Anaheim. A few of the people from the church got the approval for us to use the gymnasium to hold the event. Our first service was predictably attacked by Satan. He tried all he could to destroy what we were trying to accomplish. Just days before our event, the committee that we had established misunderstood something I said (one of my vision statements) and completely turned against me just before the event.

Unfortunately, I did not realize that these feelings were present. When it came time to set up for the event there were only about four or five people who arrived to help set-up. I remember that the pressure of setting everything up with such a small group was a bit overwhelming. I could not believe that so few of the committee showed up. It quickly became clearer that something had gone wrong. I later found out that Satan had been at work. He had taken things that I was saying in a meeting and using them to confuse a few of the people which spread to a majority of the group. It became clear later, that my words were taken out of context. However, this was all realized days after the event.

"For our struggle is not against flesh and blood, but against the rulers, against the powers, against the world forces of this darkness, against the spiritual forces of wickedness in the heavenly places." (Ephesians 6:12, NASB)

Anything Can Happen

As we begin to do God's will, we learn that many obstacles get in our way. Many of those obstacles are people's emotions and they often hinder what God is doing. As we read in Ephesians 6:12, it is not the people that we are fighting against, it is the power that is motivating the people. It is the spiritual forces that cause people to react against the work of God. My dad, Pastor Billy Karanick, has always given me good advice regarding ministry work. One of the things that he told me was to look out for "anything to happen" before a revival. Satan goes to work to try to destroy all of our plans for the ministry. This became very evident to me during this occasion. Because of this advice I knew what I was up against and was also reassured that God always prevails. It took a lot of extra work, but we were able to get the event ready just before starting time. We had put out hundreds of chairs in the gym and spent almost $3,000 for food, advertising and necessities. When the time came the band began to play and our first concert was on its way. I remember looking around in disappointment; there were only about 20-30 people in attendance. At this point, I was confident that God was in control but I knew for sure that we were fighting against powers and principalities not seen. We began the service as planned with the few that arrived. As the band continued to play it was as if the flood gates were opened. People began to arrive and within a short time, almost all the seats were filled. By the end of the night people were standing and sitting on the floor—about 400 people came to the event. Not only did God reveal His power by bringing the people, He also stirred the hearts of the people as about 100 or so responded to the invitation to accept Jesus Christ. This was a great building of our faith. We did the things that were within our ability, which was very limited, and when it came time for God to go beyond our means—He did. It reminds me of the story of the boy with the loaves and two fish.

"One of His disciples, Andrew, Simon Peter's brother, said to Him, 'There is a lad here who has five barley loaves and two fish, but what are these for so many people?' Jesus said, 'Have the people sit down.' Now there was much grass in the place. So the men sat down, in number about five thousand. Jesus then took the loaves, and having given thanks, He distributed to those who were seated; likewise also of the fish as much as they wanted. When they were filled, He said to His disciples, 'Gather up the leftover fragments so that nothing will be lost.' So they gathered them up, and filled twelve baskets with fragments from the five barley loaves which were left over by those who had eaten." (John 6:8-14, NASB)

God took what the boy had and blessed it providing more than enough to feed thousands. God was assuring us that when we do our best, He will do the rest; when we give what we can; He will provide the rest. The boy did not have enough food for so many people, but it was his willingness to give what he had (as little as it was) and Christ multiplied it. The people were full and there were leftovers. God did not provide a little; He provided abundantly.

Why did we have so many trials and troubles before this event? Because there really is a true Satan and he will try to stop anything we do for Christ. We must remember there is a greater one than Satan and that is our almighty God, the Creator, the Redeemer, and the Savior. Go through trials confidently knowing that He is always in control and the victory is His.

Man Sees the Outward, God Sees the Heart

After the amazing success of the REVIVE! event, the committee got back on track and began planning more REVIVE! events for the near future to promote our big event on July 7, 2007. We also started a campaign of calling local church pastors to find out if we could visit their church to present this vision. Some pastors said "No" right away and others put it off for later. One in particular made a statement to one of our volunteers that he felt I was too young to handle this (I think that he meant too young in the ministry) and that I may not be able to communicate the message accurately. When the committee member told me this response it was a tough blow. We had already been struggling with this new ministry and the finances; but this added just enough punch to have a negative effect on my faith and confidence that God called me to this task. Having another pastor be so negative made me wonder if I really heard from God. I know that I had it all confirmed in the beginning, but then I was starting to feel a loss of that confirmation. During this time God continued to teach me to always go back to His Word. He gives me (all of us) the answers through His Word, if I (we) will just spend time seeking those answers in His Word. I spent my time whining in prayer telling God how awful everything was going. No one was taking us seriously and I just needed to know that He had truly called me. If His own messengers (pastors) are against me and this ministry how am I supposed to be sure He called me? When I got tired of whining (finally), then I opened the Bible and He led me to

"But the LORD said to me, 'Do not say, 'I am a youth,' Because everywhere I send you, you shall go, And all that I command you, you shall speak. 'Do not be afraid of them, For I am with you to deliver you,'" declares the LORD." (Jeremiah 1:7-8, NASB)

Once again God was using the scripture to lead, teach and encourage me in the way that He wanted me to go. It truly amazes me how close God wants to be to us. He literally wants us to read His Word so He can speak to us directly. He wasn't finished talking to me on this matter. He had only confirmed that I wasn't too young and that He would give me to Words to speak. He then answered my other question just one page over in the Book of Isaiah:

"Before she travailed, she brought forth; Before her pain came, she gave birth to a boy. 'Who has heard such a thing? Who has seen such things? Can a land be born in one day? Can a nation be brought forth all at once? As soon as Zion travailed, she also brought forth her sons. 'Shall I bring to the point of birth and not

give delivery?' says the LORD. 'Or shall I who gives delivery shut the womb?' says your God.'" (Isaiah 66:7-9, NASB)

Through His Word He gave me all the assurance that I needed. He was saying that no matter what anyone says; yes, He has called me to this undertaking. No, I am not too young. Yes, He has called me to do this work and why would He take me to the time of birth and not deliver? He will see me through to the completion.

It's Not All Trials

Now, things began to take off. We had an event almost every month. The issue was that the cost for each event was running about $3,000. We wanted these concerts to be more than just a place for Christians to come and worship. We wanted the events to be more of a tool for Christians to be able to bring the unsaved. We realized that a Christian event might not really appeal to non-Christians, but we were willing to take the chance that some curious bystanders would be drawn in by the music, stay for the message and unexpectedly find their way to Christ. With that in mind, at our "Xclaimed Revive!" events we paid a local coffee vendor to offer free gourmet coffee and we also paid for Original Tommy's World Famous Hamburgers to give out free burgers and chili-cheese fries. Christians could now easily invite their unsaved friends to an exciting event which offers the hope of Salvation. Our events were completely free. I took a lot of criticism for this, but I felt adamant that I didn't want anyone to have a reason not to come. I want Christians to be able to invite their friends and say, "It's a free event. Let's go." I personally have no issue with a ministry making money in an honest fashion, but I feel any evangelistic event should be free. Yes, I probably was pushing it on the free coffee and Tommy's but that is just something I felt compelled to provide. I have a hard time imagining that some people will not hear God's Word because they can't afford admission to the event. I feel that if a person with no money to his name is walking by and hears the music or the message and wants to attend they should be able to walk right in—no money needed. Some people mentioned to me several times that I could charge a small fee like a few dollars, but I am certain that there are people who can't afford even a few dollars. I know three kids and a few homeless folks that currently come to our church that would not be able to attend the event if we charged even 50 cents. I am sure God will not judge against me because I gave His Word out for free. Based on that belief, you can see where Satan will try to attack me. Of course, Satan tried to destroy me financially, but as always, God can use those attacks as opportunities to build our trust in Jesus Christ. It wasn't long until our finances were so low that I could not pay my personal bills, like the mortgage and utilities. This was not how I planned it and I often let God know it by crying out continuously in prayer for Him to help. I am always reminded that despite what we may think at the time, He has the best ways in achieving the work that He wants to be accomplished.

"The mind of man plans his way, But the LORD directs his steps." (Proverbs 16:9, NASB)

When I originally planned all this out, I had expected the apartment to sell quickly and for us to have an excess of funds. At the present time the building was not selling and we had almost NO funds. God was taking us a completely different way than I had planned.

Fear over Faith

It was a little after midnight when my thoughts finally woke me up in fear. I have two little girls and a wife that I have to take care of and I can't even pay the utilities for our house. "God, how did I get here? I put all my faith in You and now, I am awake in the middle of the night because of fear that my family is going to be out on the streets because I tried this crazy idea." I cried, tossed and turned for about an hour because I could not sleep. I continued to pray and express my disappointment to God. What I did not realize was that God was allowing me to experience a complete dependency upon Him. He was teaching me to pray more often, read and depend upon His Word. There are different levels of faith and He was moving me up to another level. God was training me to read with the intent of getting an answer. He was establishing a foundation for a fruitful relationship. As anyone could see I had faith, but it was very little faith. I often think God would use the words He spoke to the disciples, "You of little faith" to describe me. He was equipping me to have greater faith. I often think back to this particular time in my life and realize that if God had just let the apartment building sell easily and all the funds had been provided by the proceeds, I would have missed this great opportunity of getting to know a true and living God and how much He truly cares for each of us more than we can imagine.

After hours of tossing around and a face full of tears God finally put a strong conviction on my heart to go get my Bible. Well, it was downstairs and I really did not want to get up out of bed and go get the Bible. After realizing that I wasn't going to be able to get back to sleep, I went down and got the Bible. As God has been showing me to do, I just opened it up and started reading.

"And He said to His disciples, 'For this reason I say to you, do not worry about your life, as to what you will eat; nor for your body, as to what you will put on. For life is more than food, and the body more than clothing. Consider the ravens, for they neither sow nor reap; they have no storeroom nor barn, and yet God feeds them; how much more valuable you are than the birds! And which of you by worrying can add a single hour to his life's span? If then you cannot do even a very little thing, why do you worry about other matters? Consider the lilies, how they grow: they neither toil nor spin; but I tell you, not even Solomon in all his glory clothed himself like one of these. But if God so clothes the grass in the field, which is alive today and tomorrow is thrown into the furnace, how much more will He clothe you?'" (Luke 12:22-28, NASB)

It was astounding to hear God speak through His Word, especially knowing that it was exactly what I needed to hear from Him. God was talking to me so clearly as if He was in the room with me (I know He was). After reading these verses I was overwhelmed with joy. He could not have been clearer in addressing the issues at hand. It reassured me that God was really with me in this mess. Amazingly enough, shortly after reading this scripture, I was able to go to sleep in peace. No more tears or sadness. The financial issues were still present, but now I knew that God was with me and that was enough assurance for me to be comfortable. I don't mind going through hard times, I only need to be assured that God is going with me through it all. I often aspire to having the faith of Shadrach, Meshach and Abed-nego. No matter the price of their faith, they would not waver.

Shadrach, Meshach and Abed-nego replied to the king, "O Nebuchadnezzar, we do not need to give you an answer concerning

this matter. **If it be *so,* our God whom we serve is able to deliver us from the furnace of blazing fire; and He will deliver us out of your hand, O king. But *even* if *He does* not, let it be known to you, O king, that we are not going to serve your gods or worship the golden image that you have set up.**" (Daniel 3:15-17 NASB)

As we grow in our faith, we establish a confidence in knowing that God is with us and even if we face death here on earth, we will have life eternally with the father.

Word of God Speaks—Listen Closely

Knowing that this is a spiritual battle, I should know that Satan is going to attack after a victory like this one. Sure enough, within a few days, Satan had me thinking of how in debt I really was. Going through the day I could not seem to focus on anything else but my debt. I picked up a Bible that was nearby, opened it, and began to read. Tears of overwhelming relief were rolling down my face as I realized that God had me open the Bible to Luke 12:22-28 once again. It was a great reminder of what He had told me just days ago. One of the important points that I found in this reminder, was that God had given me this same point from a different Bible. I have a few different Bibles that I use. It was a more powerful assurance of what He was telling me especially coming from a second Bible. It was not by chance that I turned to the exact same scripture—God was speaking to me just as a friend. About a week had passed and a few more bills had arrived. That was just enough to have me frustrated and overwhelmed with fear again. Once again I opened my Bible and yes, God had me turn to the same scripture again from a completely different Bible than the other two and by mere coincidence I had opened it upside down! I *love* the way that God uses these little circumstances to show that it is really Him speaking to me directly. To prove it one more time He allowed me to experience another moment from Him. It was not many days later that I went to a drive-thru at a local Mexican restaurant to order one of my favorite comfort meals, carne asada fries. After placing my order I drove up to pay and handed the cashier my ATM card. It finally happened, my account was empty. The card was denied. I told the cashier that I would go home get the money and come back. I had a few dollars in a jar at home so I returned to pay for the food. As I am sitting in the drive-thru for the second time, I felt so awful. I couldn't believe that I was this broke. My faith and strength had just taken a swift kick and I had reached another low point in my life. I could not wait to get out of this drive-thru, get home and scream! Unfortunately, there were two cars in front of me and I had to wait. This would be a great time to hear from God. I was determined to read what God was going to say to me now! I looked in the car to find my Bible (it was now becoming a habit to continually seek God's Word when I am getting spiritually beaten up) and my Bible was not in the car. I have a Bible almost everywhere; in the car, in the office, at the church, in the house and wherever else. I couldn't believe that my Bible was not here. I depended on God to help me through His Word and now His Word was not with me and I was really hating life. This was another moment where I realized that God is never out of miracles. God is in control and He never goofs up. He was about to blow my mind. There was a reason I could not find my Bible. As I am sitting in the drive-thru, feeling let down and with no way to hear from God to consult me, I turn on the radio to a local Christian radio station and, *no kidding*, the preacher is preaching on Luke 12:22-28! Inside, I busted out in hallelujahs and shouts of praise and sat in amazement and total awe. God was repeating this scripture, so that I could understand that He truly wanted me to seek His Word and rely on what it says. God was totally giving me a lesson in faith and strengthening the trust I had in Him. God really does love us and He wants us to draw closer to Him. What we see as trials are actually opportunities to see God do greater things than we could ever imagine. I feel He looks forward to revealing this to us. This is one of the greatest opportunities we have to experience an encounter with God.

"Draw near to God and He will draw near to you. Cleanse your hands, you sinners; and purify your hearts, you double-minded." (James 4:8, NASB)

Become Very Acquainted—Communicate

God does not need us to accomplish anything; He is God. He allows us the opportunity to be part of His great work and uses these opportunities for us to grow in our confidence and faith in Him. I found that as God led us through the trials and struggles that I was praying and reading my Bible continuously. I was growing closer to Him and He was drawing closer to me. It became a necessity for me to be able to stay sane. I would pray and read the Bible to find the answer that God would reveal to me. It was such an awesome thing to communicate with God. Eventually, Satan began trying harder and harder to send attacks on me and my family. Nights became the place that Satan really seemed to mentally attack me with issues so that I could not sleep well. I would worry about all the things that were going out of my control. To my rescue, God provides! "Faith Comes By Hearing" is a company that distributes audio Bibles throughout the world. They had sent free CD's to our church and I downloaded the entire New Testament to my MP3 player. What another astounding blessing from God. Since Satan attacked at night, I found that playing the Bible on my MP3 player throughout the night set my mind at ease and each night I would sleep more peacefully. Hearing God's Word was powerful. The Bible is more than a book of words. It is a book of Life, full of meaning and meant to be the guide for our lives—it is God's Word.

Growing Together in Faith

The one thing I was neglecting to do was to include my wife. I realized that I was building this great prayer time with God, but my wife wasn't experiencing it like I was because I had not included her in the process. I felt like I would be protecting her by not including her in all the issues. She obviously realized the battles that were taking place, but as a husband, I felt it was better not to overload her with all the details. However, by doing so, I was keeping her from seeing the amazing miracles that God was working. She did not get to truly experience the complete helplessness that I felt and then the completely miraculous work that God would do to bring us through it all. God uses these times for us to grow stronger and I was keeping her away from that opportunity. She needed to walk through this with me so that we could both grow together and grow stronger. She obviously had her own prayer time, but I felt we should be growing together in these experiences. We began to pray together and I was able to see her faith increase and her ability to see God's amazing work in our lives. This was a major change for my wife. Before we were married she had a very financially stable life. Now, she was married to a Jesus freak who had spent all their money on a Christian concert and was having a hard time making it succeed. Husbands and wives need to remember that they are not alone in their marriage. The spouse should be involved in the good and bad times so that you will both grow together. Once Christina and I began praying together more often our strength and faith seemed to be more on the same level. I remember several nights that she could not sleep because of all the things that were happening. She would wake me up in the middle of the night and say, "Let's pray." We would pray and she was then able to go back to sleep. Satan would love to use these occasions to separate us, keep us from communicating and dissolve our marriage, but God strengthens and confirms our relationship to Him and to each other.

It wasn't long until Satan was trying another angle to get us to stop this ministry. He began to attack my family. My daughter was diagnosed with lead poisoning. After weeks of prayer, God not only revealed the source of the lead, but also healed my daughter from the poison. Not long afterwards, my daughter's baby teeth began to decay. We found that her teeth had no enamel and she would eventually have to have surgery to fix and cap her teeth. We spent a major part of our time looking for a dentist that we trusted and worked with young children (under 2 years old). Once we found a dentist we were comfortable with, we found that the surgery had to be done at a hospital and the cost was going to be over $20,000. It was like Satan continued to attack us financially and now he was trying to attack my daughter's health. Just as He did previously, God provided everything. After all was said and done we only had to come up with about $2,000. Normally, dental care is not covered by medical insurance but due to the circumstances our insurance company paid for everything (the surgery, medications, etc.) except the dentist. The fascinating thing is that the dentist had mentioned that he had recently submitted a request for a similar case to the same insurance and the family was denied any coverage because it was dental and not medical. I am very aware that God had His hand in this matter on our behalf.

The more I see what is happening the more I realize that everything that I was so willing to turn over to God is exactly what Satan really attacks. We had given our lives and our finances; these are the two places Satan attacked the most. Ironically, it is where God made us the strongest. As we needed it, He provided us with scripture and strength.

The Faith of a Mustard Seed

"And He said to them, 'Because of the littleness of your faith; for truly I say to you, if you have faith the size of a mustard seed, you will say to this mountain, 'Move from here to there,' and it will move; and nothing will be impossible to you.'" (Matthew 17:20, NASB)

Growing up, I remembered this verse because it was used frequently within the church. I was often disappointed because I would pray for something and I would not receive what I prayed for from God. I felt that at the very least, I had a "mustard seed" amount of faith. Based on the way I and others interpreted this verse I should be able to pray and with my small amount of faith see some results. So many people are led astray from the Bible because they read it assuming the interpretation, and when it doesn't work the way that they felt it should go, then they make another assumption that the Bible is wrong. The Bible has never been proven wrong because it is never wrong. However, many times we interpret it incorrectly. In all cases we should look for God's guidance for the correct interpretation. It is not the mere fact of having a small amount of faith that will move mountains; it is fact that God can work with a small amount of faith and make it grow into a greater amount of faith. With that faith, which grew from a small amount into a fully developed amount of faith, nothing is impossible. The critical point is that you must have at least a little faith for God to work with. When we first began the ministry we had enough faith to give about $50,000 or so, thinking that we would have money left over from the sale of the property. God allowed events to take place to strengthen our faith. God knew that I did not have enough faith at that time to spend over $200,000, face multiple foreclosures, family health issues, people's criticisms, and many other trials. God was willing to take what I had and make it grow. It is amazing to see how God works in our lives.

Faith in God or Money?

One of my most frustrating issues has been the lack of faith among so many church leaders. I would often be approached by church leaders asking, "How would you accomplish this event if you do not have the funding?" or "Why don't you consider doing a smaller event?" It amazes me that even within the church people have supposedly focused their faith on God, but that faith is solely dependent upon how much money they have access to. It reminds me of the story of the woman in the Bible who washed Jesus feet with the very expensive perfume, it was worth about a year's salary, and people could not understand why she would waste this perfume on Jesus feet.

"Mary then took a pound of very costly perfume of pure nard, and anointed the feet of Jesus and wiped His feet with her hair; and the house was filled with the fragrance of the perfume. But Judas Iscariot, one of His disciples, who was intending to betray Him, said, 'Why was this perfume not sold for three hundred denarii and given to poor *people*?'" (John 12:3-5, NASB)

Today, many people in the church still seem to question why people do extraordinary things for Christ. I am here to confess that you cannot out give God. I feel the church needs to be the example of faith and commitment to God's Word. The Bible says to walk by faith not by sight. We should be the first in line to do just that and provide evidence of God's ability to prevail. To walk by faith means that we do not know how it will all come together, but we know it will come together for the glory of God.

My answer to anyone asking those questions is still the same, "God called us to do this and He will provide ALL our needs. In a manner of speaking, I am His employee and this is His event. The debt is His and He will provide. We are to be good stewards, but we are not to live in fear or to doubt His abilities to do the impossible. The reason that we did not organize a smaller event was because God did not call us to do that. He gave us the vision and the locations. We followed His lead not ours. I serve a true and living God. If it were not so then I should be very fearful for my actions, but I am certain of the One that has called me and once again, He will provide."

In Moments of Doubt

During one of my moments of doubt where I really needed to be encouraged, I was driving the car and my two girls were listening to the newest Veggie Tales DVD. I obviously could not watch it while I was driving, but I could listen. They began to tell a story of a man that owned an orphanage who never seemed to have enough money to run it. Every time they needed anything He would pray and God would always supply the need for the orphanage. The helpers came to him and said we don't have any food. He says, "You know what we have to do; pray." Someone knocks on the door and it is a person that had a burden on their heart during the night that the orphanage would need food, so they stayed up all night cooking bread and brought it to the door. I could hardly believe what I was hearing. It was exactly what I had been telling people, "Let's be an example and live like we are serving a true and loving God. If we say we believe He is real; let's live it!" I went home and told my dad about the DVD. I said to him that I was encouraged by a cartoon; however it was exactly what I needed to hear. He replied, "That was not just a story from a cartoon, it was a true story about a man name George Muller and he really did run an orphanage daily depending on God to provide." This was so motivating to hear that this was a true story. I loved the fact that someone lived out the faith and was a true witness for what God can do in all of our lives. I wish that the church body could live more like Muller. I needed to see how God really works and that was a great example. I see so many religions worshiping different gods in this world and it is about time we prove that ours is the only true God by living out our faith. The Bible is true, God is real and we can live our lives as proof when we are dependent upon Him and His strength. Our faith should always be in Him and not in money. Too many Christians have faith in money over faith in God. The problem with many churches today is that they have faith in the person at the church who has the most money. Preachers do not always preach the message as directly as it should be, but only because the pastor did not want to offend his big tithers. I would rather fear God than anything that the wealthiest person on earth can do to my life.

Revelation of Faith

My faith, in the beginning, seemed to be very strong. That was until God revealed the truth. What I called "faith in God" turned out to be "when the building sells the money from the sale will be used for the event" faith. My faith was actually in the building. When the building sells everything will be OK. God spent a lot of time pointing this out. He may have spent so much time on it because I wasn't getting it. Who knows? For whatever reason, I finally did get it and it was very clear. My faith had been in the value of the building and not as much in God's amazing power. God knew that I was convinced that if the apartment building would sell, everything would be OK. God redirected my faith to trusting in Him, even if the apartment building did not sell, I can trust in Him to provide. God is in the relationship building business. He wants us to trust Him and realize that He supplies our needs and takes care of us which in return proves that He is alive and is truly real. God used this time to strengthen our faith and ability to trust in Him alone.

What's a Credit Rating Anyway?

It seemed everything was finally in place. My wife and I are fully devoted to this project and we are waiting for the sale of the property. We began our advertising campaign, the "Revive!" services and other things that cost money. Eventually, we had used most of our savings and the property still hadn't sold. At this point I had a really good credit rating and I knew that my mortgage payment was coming due and we did not have the ability to pay. I prayed in faith that God would not let me miss this payment and would allow the building to sell so that we could use the proceeds to survive and pay for the event. Credit is so hard to keep in good standing and I was proud of the fact that mine was good. When the deadline for the payment came there was no miraculous sign from God or anything. Nope, I just missed my payment and it just about destroyed me with disappointment and sadness. This was a hard thing to accept. This was one of God's greatest lessons for me to learn. I realized through this that I was in a real battle. I was a servant for Christ trying to save the lost. Satan, a true enemy of God, is going to attack any way that he can; especially the things that I am most proud of in my life. It is as if God wanted to wake me up and show me that this stuff is real! We need to be prepared to fight a real battle as true soldiers for Christ.

If I choose to fight the fight I must realize there is an enemy and God revealed that to me. He also tried my faith. I had to make a choice to continue this mission or to get out. I had to realize that I may lose everything I have. In this case, was it worth losing everything, to accomplish what God had called me to do as His servant? The Bible is clear that we are not to love the things of this world. I know people hate to hear this but the truth is, our finances and credit rating are also things of this world and if we put them above God (if they interfere with God's work) then we must reassess our thinking. I am not saying to ignore paying bills, but don't let the bills become the reason for not serving God completely. Realize that you will be attacked in all parts of our life. Be ready to be humbled by what you believe.

God, Will You Please Answer Me?

The inevitable happened. We had missed about three months of payments, all our funds had dried up and we were literally living day-by-day. I had been called to go speak at a Korean youth camp up high in the mountains outside of Los Angeles. My calling is to evangelize, so no matter what is happening in my life I know that I am to obey God. Even though the house is now facing foreclosure I am sure that I am to go to the camp. For three days, I preached and for three days and nights I prayed, read the Bible continuously and cried inside and outside. God was with me even through the pain. However, I wasn't hearing from Him. I was seeking that comforting Word that only He can give. My finances at home were constantly on my mind and I needed God to give me direction. I also was not able to hear from my family. I was in the mountains with no phone and no communication. I would pray for God to just answer me that everything is going to be OK. That He is in this with me and my family and that my family and home are going to be fine. I would read the Bible for hours, but He just did not seem to answer my prayer. After three days of praying he still did not answer. I was fairly disappointed and very depressed by this time. I had prayed that God would make it clear to me that He was in control, but still nothing. I read the Bible more intently than ever before. I had to find His answer. I finally understood the verse that says to ask, seek and knock. I needed to ask, seek and knock. In the past, God had provided Scripture for me fairly easily, but here He was truly making me seek His answer. I had prayed, cried, begged, and continually read the Bible looking for His response. I was determined to seek God's Word and let Him lead me to the answer.

The camp was over and I was waiting for my wife to come pick me up. As I sat on the highest steps looking over into the open-air church, I continued reading the Bible and I read from John, "Anything you ask in my name I will do it." Well, God, that is what I need to hear, but it is a little too late.

"Whatever you ask in My name, that will I do, so that the Father may be glorified in the Son. If you ask Me anything in My name, I will do it." (John 14:13-14, NASB)

I have been begging for three days now that you give me an answer. I could have used that a few days ago. But, now I need more. I need to be sure that you are in this and taking care of me and my family. I continued to read and once again a different verse in John saying the same thing, *"Anything you ask in my name I will do it"* appeared. OK God, that makes me feel a little better since you seemed to have stated it twice. I continued to read and it was like the words just kept jumping out at me, "Anything you ask in my name I will do it." About five times within a few pages. God continues to tell me that He will answer all my requests. Anything I ask in His name! Finally, I get it! Everything is going to be OK. God was teaching me to trust Him even more than I have ever had to trust Him and it was not an easy task. It was like boot camp. This is not like regular boot camp; this is like the Special Forces boot camp. God truly is preparing us for something great. I told my wife the whole story as we were headed home.

When we got home nothing seemed to be any different except we knew that God had given us His word and we knew that He would not fail.

A few days later, two of my friends, out of the blue, offered to loan us the money to make our mortgage payments. We were in the beginning stages of foreclosure so there were extra fees on top of our regular payment and they loaned us the money to pay everything. God really came through for us and we were just swept away by His amazing promise and the fulfillment of His promise to us. Still, God wasn't finished. His plan was not to just help me with the loan but to strengthen our faith once again. *He had taught me to pray asking for His help, read the Bible seeking His answer, and then have faith in him that He will do what He says.* Yes, God had completed what He said. Now, it was time to reinforce it with great confidence. We are out of the foreclosure process, but we still are having a problem keeping up the payments. God provided us enough money to pay my friends back and then we struggled with the next mortgage payments. I really began to question God about these amazing trials that we are facing. Why would you rescue us from foreclosure just to allow us to go back into foreclosure again? I felt like the Israelites during the exit from Egypt. They continued to question God after every miracle.

"Therefore the people quarreled with Moses and said, "Give us water that we may drink." And Moses said to them, "Why do you quarrel with me? Why do you test the LORD?" But the people thirsted there for water; and they grumbled against Moses and said, 'Why, now, have you brought us up from Egypt, to kill us and our children and our livestock with thirst.'" (Exodus 17:2-3, NASB)

Road to Foreclosure

It wasn't long until, once again, our house was not only in foreclosure but was about to go to be sold in the foreclosure sale. This obviously had taken many months and my wife and I had been through many mixed feelings about what God had in store for us and our future.

There was a point where Christina had had enough. She was ready to throw in the towel. Our finances never seemed to be right, the event was never completely sound, our children had been sick and God at times just seemed too far away. I remember asking her to get into the car and we went for a drive. She could scream, yell, cry or anything she wanted to do as I drove to nowhere in particular. I finally pulled over into a parking lot, turned off the car and confirmed with her that we can stop anytime she is ready. I can get a regular job, call off the event and start fresh with no great expectations. We are in this together or we are out of it together. She replied, "I fear stepping out of the will of God more than I do losing all that we own." It was that confidence in Christ that kept us moving forward. Just as God had wanted the Israelites to do, God wanted my wife and me to do—put all our trust in Him. He had shown us not many months ago that He could and would take care of us. It was a painful learning experience but He knew that the reward was great.

Our home was scheduled to go to foreclosure sale on Monday. (It is now Friday.) I knew that this was detrimental not only for me and my family but also for the ministry. If the home is lost in foreclosure we would have no way to continue the ministry. During the past few months God had really worked with us in strengthening our faith and we understood that our faith was in Him and not these circumstances. We were troubled by the situation, but our faith was greater than our fear. This became apparent when we received the notice that the sale was for Monday. We had both come to the point of completely depending on God and realizing that we could not do anything. It was all out of our hands. Nevertheless, there was such a comforting feeling knowing that everything was going to be OK. This was our greatest confirmation that God had advanced us to new heights. We truly have grown in our faith. God is in complete control and we are fine with it being this way. It happened that besides being Associate Pastor, I was also the bus driver for our church and on Friday the church was scheduled for our annual beach trip to San Diego, California about 2 hours away from our church. Knowing that I would have nowhere to live on Monday I took the church on the trip as scheduled anyways.

"And as you go, preach, saying, 'The kingdom of heaven is at hand.' Heal *the* sick, raise *the* dead, cleanse *the* lepers, cast out demons. Freely you received, freely give. Do not acquire gold, or silver, or copper for your money belts, or a bag for *your* journey, or even two coats, or sandals, or a staff; for the worker is worthy of his support." (Matthew 10:7-10, NASB)

My wife and I were both so confident that God would take care of us that we had not even begun to pack up the house. His Word says that the worker is worthy of support and we stand by that promise. We were dedicated to doing what God had called us to do, and we weren't sitting at home being lazy or avoiding our obligations. We were taking the path that Christ had directed us to go and we were confident that He would provide our needs just as He said to His disciples in Matthew 10:10. It was a confidence we had never experienced before. While I was at the beach with the church, I would be a little social, but for the most part I was walking alone praying, asking God to send help really soon. As I was walking and praying my two friends I mentioned earlier, once again out of the blue, called me on my cell phone. "So how is it going with your house?" I replied, "It's going to sale on Monday."

They immediately said, "We can't let you lose your house. Give us your account number we will wire the money to them directly!" I wasn't sure how God was going to answer this one but I was confident that no matter the outcome He was taking us wherever we needed us to be. The result was an even greater confirmation of faith and dependency on Him. I can't fully express how important it is for God to allow us the opportunity to experience these trials and tribulations so that we not only grow our faith, but we also get a greater glimpse of who He is and His irrefutable abilities. I can look back now and see how much God really loved us and how He would go with us through every situation and by doing so He revealed to us that He is real, alive and well. The outcome of putting all your hope and faith in Him is confirmation that He does exist and is a prominent part of your life. Once you experience this type of relationship you will no longer question—"Is there a God?" Not only will you see God in your life you will see that He genuinely cares for you. Throughout these past few months there were numerous times that I wanted out. It was a combination of feelings while going through all the variety of issues. I remember thinking how good it would be to go back to my old life (just a year or so ago), to have good credit, be self-employed, and with little worries in comparison. Obviously, that wasn't God's plan. He could see the future and He could see that these hard times for a little while would result in a strong lasting relationship with Him for my entire family. Now, I am thankful that He did not allow me to quit.

Faith of a Small Plant

I was now in a place of confusion. God had saved our home and allowed us to continue, but that didn't answer the more obvious question, "How are we going to pay for this event? The apartment isn't selling and we do not have any money." It is obvious that our relationship with God is stronger and that we have seen His amazing work in our own lives. However, just as the Israelites, Peter and most of all mankind did, we almost always fall back to our fear and lose hope. I believe that is why God takes so much time and allows so many different obstacles to get in our path along the way. He knows that it takes repetition for us to break our old ways and begin new ways. He wants us to aspire to an unwavering faith in all situations. As clear as it was that we had a greater faith than ever before, I believe we were at the point somewhere in the middle with our faith. We were no longer a mustard seed, but we were not a full grown mature plant either.

One night, I needed some answers and somewhere around 9 p.m. I took one of my notorious drives around town so I could be alone with Jesus and really tell Him my true feelings. I pulled into a parking lot and continued praying. "God, are we in this alone? Are you going to help us or is this it?" No matter how many miracles God had done for us, I just could not completely grasp the fact that this would all work out in His time. I needed my daily supply of reassurance, and God made it clear once again. I turned on my radio while in the parking lot. I listen to the Christian station as usual expecting God to speak to me and boy did He ever. The preacher was preaching from Deuteronomy 8.

"All the commandments that I am commanding you today you shall be careful to do, that you may live and multiply, and go in and possess the land which the LORD swore *to give* to your forefathers. You shall remember all the way which the LORD your God has led you in the wilderness these forty years, that He might humble you, testing you, to know what was in your heart, whether you would keep His commandments or not. He humbled you and let you be

hungry, and fed you with manna which you did not know, nor did your fathers know, that He might make you understand that man does not live by bread alone, but man lives by everything that proceeds out of the mouth of the LORD." (Deuteronomy 8:1-3, NASB)

This is the chapter where God is speaking to the Israelites and assuring them that He would get them into the Promised Land and they were going to be amazed. The food and water are plentiful and they are to eat and enjoy it. Once they are done they are commanded by God to remember Him and give Him thanks. Yes, this is the one place in the Bible that speaks of eating and then after eating praying and thanking God for the food. For me this was exactly what I had asked in my prayer. I had begged God to reassure me, and that is what He did with this passage of Scripture. This was His reply that He was taking us all the way into this ministry outreach and when He has done it; we are to remember that it was Him who supplied everything and made it possible for us. We need to remember to thank Him after we have enjoyed the victory. Most of all, there will be victory!

Sale of the Apartment

Finally! An offer for the apartment came in and it was lower than we needed. A lot of negotiating got a little more but we would end up short of what we expected—very short. Time was getting closer and we were well behind schedule. We accepted the offer and near the end of November the property closed escrow. Throughout our trials and financial situation we had been working with the production company regarding the details of the event. I called to give them the great news that we had the money for the band deposits and other initial items. I sensed a different tone in his voice as he paused and then said that they were no longer going to be able to produce our event because they now had another event scheduled on the same day in Colorado. I wasn't sure what to think. It definitely was not as transparent as they may claim. After all these ups and downs that we had been through, we were now ready to go and as it turns out this guy had been looking at other events all along. We had spoken during these past few months about the band lineup that we would have for the day. Supposing that we still had these bands I figured that even if we lose this company we would still be able to put together the event. Now, I need to make a decision quickly. The Arrowhead Pond of Anaheim (now named the HONDA Center) has our event date on hold but, I needed to bring them $25,000 deposit within the next few days. After a few hours I realized that we only have six months to put this event together from scratch and with a team of volunteers that have good hearts but little experience. The possibility that we could pull this off is slim. I met with the representative from the Arrowhead Pond and cancelled the date.

Event Cancelled

It was official; we did not have a venue, a production company, or an event. It was a feeling of complete loss of hope. I did not feel like we had failed, but more like we had done all we could and we had just reached a place where we needed others to have faith along with us but that wasn't the case. When Jesus went back to his home town He said that the reason He did not do any miracles was due to their lack of faith.

"And He did not do many miracles there because of their unbelief."
(Matthew 13:58, NASB)

I just felt that without others having faith it just wasn't going to happen. After a day or so of asking God how we ended up here, with all the volunteers that had gone through this rollercoaster ride along with my wife and me, shouldn't they see something better than this? We had just sold the apartment building and now we have some money but we don't have anything else. God did not seem to reply at this point.

There is a production company up in Northern California that was producing an event at Knott's Berry Farm in Buena Park, California. I called the owner and met with him and a few of his production managers. I wanted to run our idea by him and see what he thought. He seemed genuinely concerned and would have probably assisted us except for his current schedule and some personal family circumstances that he needed to be involved in. However, his son and one of the managers offered to assist us if we needed anything from them.

During these eventful and stressful times of the last month I overlooked paying the insurance for our church. Since I really did not have anything else to do, I drove the payment to the company. It was a nice drive to Pasadena, California about an hour from Anaheim. After making the payment I realized that I was close to the Rose Bowl Stadium. I am not sure why but I picked up my cell phone and called the stadium. I left a message for the representative. On Wednesday, I was walking into the District office for our church when I received a return phone call from the Rose Bowl. I told her the story about the recent event failure and that I was thinking of having a smaller event. Then I asked her if they rented out the Rose Bowl parking lot? My thought was to have a small concert in the parking lot. She confirmed that the Rose Bowl would rent out the parking lot and the cost was $10,000. My first thought was that we could afford to do this. My second thought was how soon can we get a contract together? She said that we could meet sometime next week and I replied, "How about tomorrow?" She agreed and I was off to the Rose Bowl the next day. I seriously don't know what I am doing or why I feel we can put together a concert in the parking lot of the Stadium. I met with her and her manager and we took a short tour of the area. We then walked into the stadium. I remember walking toward the field and thinking to myself, "I am about to walk on the field of the Rose Bowl Stadium—this is so cool!" The manager asked, "Why don't you rent the stadium instead of the parking lot?" That would be awesome but we can't afford the whole Stadium. I remember his next words exactly, "Billy Graham preached here; you should be inside here too. I will give it to you for the same cost as the cost of the parking lot." He continued with an excellent thought. The Rose Bowl has an annual 4th of July orchestra and firework show. He said that they would leave the stage up for a few extra days and we could use it instead of having to get our own stage. I could not believe it, I felt like I should look for a halo and wings on this guy. It did not take me long to figure out that I wanted to do this.

I called up everyone and told them that the vision continues and we have about six months to put it all together. Seriously, the worst thing that could happen now is I could be out $10,000. We have just a little time to learn how to do this, contact the bands and put it all together. I don't know why exactly, but I felt great. Everything was going to work out OK.

After a few weeks, I felt the urge to go back to all the pastors and let them know the updated plan. I have had better thoughts in my life and this was not one of them. I went to the next pastors meeting and began to tell the exciting news. It wasn't long until the same pastor from the other meetings added his opinion once again. "Well, Paul, is it fair to say that your vision has changed from when you first started? It's OK if it has. I just wanted to see where you stand." The truth is that he has been against this from the beginning. Every time I mention this event he has lots of insulting questioning. Recently, one of the ladies that prepare the bulletin at his church put in a prayer request for Xclaimed Ministries. When this pastor saw it he had her remove it. He said that it was going to fail so we are not going to pray for it. During this pastor's meeting I finally had enough with people attacking and belittling the idea that we had worked so hard for to obey God's calling. I will be the first to admit that I should not have lost my temper, but I did. I have almost lost my home, destroyed my credit, watched a production company painlessly turn their back on us, faced a possible lawsuit over the rights of the name Xclaimed, surrendered everything to God to walk by faith not by sight, sought God's answers and witnessed God's amazing miracles for the ministry and my family and now, to hear someone that had not even lifted a thoughtful word towards this ministry—I responded very rudely. After realizing what I was doing I calmed the situation down and completed my announcement (I am fairly certain that my announcement did not go over so well). I called the pastor and a majority of the others and apologized for my sarcasm and rudeness.

There was another pastor's meeting and Dr. Doane asked the Pastors to pray for me. Dr. Doane placed his hand on my shoulder as they prayed. As the prayer began, I felt one other hand placed on my back. It meant a lot to me that one of the other pastors would at the least; support me in prayer and laying on of hands. After the meeting was over, I asked Dr. Doane, "Who was the other pastor that came up and layed hands on me?" He replied, "No one else came up." I was sure that someone came up and it was possible that Dr. Doane missed them.

On my way home, I called one of the other pastors and asked him the same question; he gave me the same answer, "No one came up to you." I *know* there was a hand that touched me while we were praying and I have little doubt that it was any other than God giving me one more confirmation that He is with me. I can never prove it and I don't need to. It's between me and God—I want to keep it that way.

Days later I met with my newly structured volunteer production group and we began putting the event together. Right away we began to contact the management companies for the bands that we had scheduled for the Arrowhead Pond to let them know that we will be moving the event to the Rose Bowl Stadium in Pasadena, California. It wasn't long before we realized that the previous production company from Orange County had booked all the bands in their own name instead of our name and as you may have guessed, they are all lined up for the event in Colorado. Now, we have a problem, we have a great location at an affordable cost and no bands for the lineup. I had no clue that this production company was taking the lineup of bands that we had. Once again, I simply turned it over to God and said this is Your event. You are in control. We later found out that there were only a handful of bands left to choose from because so many bands were signed up for the event in Colorado. Within a few weeks we had a list of bands from which we selected Skillet, Leeland, The Afters, KJ-52, Warren Barfield, and Decyfer Down. Finally, we have a location, the bands and the money. Our newly revised estimated cost of the entire day was nearly $100,000.

My wife and I originally figured the event would cost approximately $50,000. However, with our estimates from the Arrowhead Pond event we were looking at roughly $300,000. So now, to have it at $100,000 we are looking good. We began advertising the event with posters and handouts to local churches. Eventually, we were putting it on the radio through Los Angeles, Orange County, and the Inland Empire. We met up with the Orange County radio station and found they would not run our advertisement because of a contract that they have with the production company that produces their yearly concert festival in Irvine, California (Yes, the same production company that deserted us for our event). They created a block-out of any advertising of concerts in the area for a 90-day period before the event. The only event advertising on the station is for their own event. Since they dominate the Orange County area we were not able to get great coverage in the OC.

God blessed us in other ways which gave us the opportunity to work with the radio station in the Inland Empire. AIR1 is just unbelievable in their ministry as a radio station. The Bible tells us that we can know a tree by its fruit. Air1 not only plays Christian music, but they read Scripture, they pray with people on the air, they have pastors readily available to take calls and pray with anyone around the clock and most of all they talk about Jesus out loud on the air without reservation. When we called them for advertising, they helped us as a ministry and made it so easy for us to reach the lost. They truly are in this for the same purpose and not just for making money for themselves. As I have always believed, it is OK to make money but never put money above God. Seek His purpose first and He will provide the rest. Air-1 puts Christ first and the fruit of their ministry shows it well

I received a call to meet with the management at the Rose Bowl. The terms for the Rose Bowl had to be changed. They could no longer offer us the stage that they had offered originally. This causes a huge financial problem. This is now going to increase our cost almost $40,000. That was followed by additional bad news. The Rose Bowl representative was going to limit our attendance to 8,000 people otherwise we would have additional charges per person allowed to enter the gate. We negotiated and agreed to increase the limit to 10,000 people before any additional cost. To add to the misery he had made a scheduling error. The Swap meet is scheduled for that Sunday morning so we have to be out by 2 a.m. Sunday morning. The event is scheduled to be over at 10:00 p.m. That does not give us a lot of time to remove all the sound and lighting equipment and tear down a stage.

We also received a revised cost which just about ended the event. We were being charged for so many additional items you would have thought that we were having a sporting event with a full stadium. There were costs for an exorbitant amount of police, fire, paramedics, isle attendants, custodial personnel and the list kept going! We contested it to no avail. Contractually, they was no limit to the amount of people they could hire for this event. After the event, they finally admitted they had too many people; unfortunately, we had already paid for them.

On July 2, 2007, I was crazy enough to be working at our annual firework stand for our church fundraiser. I received a call from the Rose Bowl folks explaining that they realized that they believed we needed to hire more staff for the event and we would need to bring in additional funds. With the increase, we now needed to bring in $34,990 by the afternoon. If I had a mirror, I would have seen that I had probably lost all color in my face and was probably sheet white. Just five days before the event and now, we are faced with this. With fierce negotiating, I was able to postpone the time to July 5 at noon. The Rose Bowl Management was adamant that if the funds were not there by noon they would cancel the event. I woke up on the morning of July 5th and was exhausted from spending the last few days in the fireworks stand and from trying to raise the additional money needed for the event. Since I was unable to raise the additional funds, I just laid in bed and prayed for about an hour. I remember saying to God that we are just days two days away from the event and if this is how it ends that it is fine, but I have no reason to get out of bed. I have sacrificed everything that I have and I can't do anymore. After crying my heart out, I finally felt a great peace about the whole endeavor and got out of bed. I felt that everything is fine no matter what happens and that we fought a good fight to do what we could to reach the lost. I walked downstairs to find my wife and others were counting the money from the fireworks stand. Christina looks at me and says, "How much money did we need for the Rose Bowl?" I replied, "$34,990." She said, "We just counted, $35,000 (and some change) from the fireworks stand." This was one of our greatest years on fireworks sales. I have been so pre-occupied with the event I didn't realize our sales. I called all the church board members and they unanimously agreed to donate the funds to the event. It was approaching noon, so I called the Rose Bowl Stadium and said that I am on my way and I am coming in with cash.

Two Types of Faith

Jesus uses the mustard seed in His illustrations of faith.

"And the Lord said, 'If you had faith like a mustard seed, you would say to this mulberry tree, 'Be uprooted and be planted in the sea'; and it would obey you." (Luke 17:6, NASB)

He also says, **". . . if you have faith the size of a mustard seed, you will say to this mountain, 'Move from here to there,' and it will**

move; and nothing will be impossible to you." (Matthew 17:19-20, NASB)

My first question in my interest in growing in faith was to understand what the importance of the mustard seed is. In this case, it may have been answered in another parable of Christ, **"He presented another parable to them, saying, "The kingdom of heaven is like a mustard seed, which a man took and sowed in his field; and this is smaller than all other seeds, but when it is full grown, it is larger than the garden plants and becomes a tree, so that the birds of the air come and nest in its branches."** (Matthew 13:31-32, NASB)

The mustard seed, which is about the size of this dot (.), grows into an extremely large plant; so large that the birds can nest in it. I know that I have the gift of faith, but I wasn't clear as to what that actually meant until I put my faith to the test. Basically, it was when I accepted the call to put on the Xclaimed 777 outreach concert at the Rose Bowl Stadium. I believe that all Christians have some amount of faith. It is an essential element to being a Christian because we are saved through faith.

"For by grace you have been saved through faith; and that not of yourselves, *it is* the gift of God;" (Ephesians 2:8, NASB)

Hence, we as Christians have a small amount of faith. Now, we need to build upon that faith. I see two distinctive types of faith. One is saving faith and the other is living faith. Saving faith is the faith that emphasizes the acknowledgement of Jesus as God and our redeemer. By faith, we know that Christ died on the cross and paid the price for our sins; a price that we could not pay; God Himself came down to us and paid the price. Paul repeats the words of Christ, "**. . . to open their eyes so that they may turn from darkness to light and from the dominion of Satan to God, that they may receive forgiveness of sins and an inheritance among those who have been sanctified by faith in Me.**'" (Acts 25:18, NASB)

It is by faith in Christ that we are freed from sin. To have faith in Jesus Christ means to believe in His Word. John 1:1 says, that in the beginning was the Word (Christ) and the Word was with God. This reveals two separate identities; for something to be *with* something then there must be two. So Jesus is separate from God. However, the verse continues and says that the Word (Christ) was God. This reveals that Jesus is God. This verse clarifies part of the Trinity, that Jesus is God, but that He is capable of being separate; explaining the ability to come to earth as Christ. As confusing as this may seem, the easiest way to understand this is to put it into the correct perspective. Jesus is God, but He is not the Father; The Father is God, but He is not the Son; the Holy Spirit is God, but He is not the Father or the Son—all three make up one God not three Gods (as some may suggest). An egg has three parts, the white, yolk, and shell; they are all three separate parts, but together they make up the complete egg. Having faith in Jesus for salvation means that we believe in Jesus; even, when He says that He is the only way to the Father (John 14:6). Jesus did not claim that He was *a* way to the Father; He said He was *the* way to the Father. There is no other way to Heaven except through Christ. That is the faith that is required to be saved.

The apostle Paul speaks of the saving faith when he says, "**. . . nevertheless knowing that a man is not justified by the works of the Law but through faith in Christ Jesus, even we have believed in**

Christ Jesus, so that we may be justified by faith in Christ and not by the works of the Law; since by the works of the Law no flesh will be justified." (Galatians 2:16, NASB)

Paul is clarifying that you cannot work for your salvation; there is nothing that a person can do to obtain salvation except through faith in Jesus Christ. It is a gift, it is not worked for; it is simply accepted by us from Christ.

On the contrary, James speaks of faith, **"For just as the body without the spirit is dead, so also faith without works is dead."** (James 2:26, NASB)

Many people see this as a discrepancy between Paul and James, but that it not the case at all. Paul is speaking of "saving faith" while James is speaking of "living faith" (a walk of faith). Paul also addresses this as **"Walking by faith."** (2 Corinthians 5:7, NASB) Once we are saved through faith, we need to walk by faith. Live the life of faith. This is the works resulting from our faith. If I believe in Christ, then I should do the things that He calls me to do. Lifting weights builds muscle and ultimately strengthens the body. Unfortunately, muscles that are not used are not strengthened and become weak. Faith is like the muscle, if it is exercised, it will strengthen; otherwise, it will weaken. James claims that without the work of your faith; faith is dead. Jesus says to His disciples, "Do you still have no faith?" As the wind is tossing the sea, the boat that the disciples are in is about to sink, Jesus calms the sea and then asks the disciples, "Do you still have no faith?"

"And there arose a fierce gale of wind, and the waves were breaking over the boat so much that the boat was already filling up. Jesus Himself was in the stern, asleep on the cushion; and they woke Him

and said to Him, 'Teacher, do You not care that we are perishing?' And He got up and rebuked the wind and said to the sea, 'Hush, be still.' And the wind died down and it became perfectly calm. And He said to them, 'Why are you afraid? Do you still have no faith?'" (Mark 4:37-39, NASB)

It could appear that Jesus is harsh with them in the face of what they perceive was their impending doom. Jesus was not being harsh, but He was broadening their growth in faith. The disciples had seen some amazing miracles through Christ and yet, they were still fearful even though He is with them. He wants them to realize that they need not fear because He is with them.

Faith Inauguration

To walk by faith means to place your life in the hands of Christ. Many people comment that Jesus is their co-pilot, but when you truly put your life in the hands of Christ you are placing Jesus as the pilot of your life, not as co-pilot. The goal is to give Christ full control of your life, but it takes time and relationship building to get to the place to turn full control over to Him. That is one reason Jesus used the illustration of the mustard seed. The seed is so small, but with time and nurturing, that seed will grow large and healthy. It will grow to a point that not only is it strong and powerful within itself, but it can also help others. Jesus said that the mustard seed would grow into a tree and that the birds could nest in it.

First of all, we as Christians must have some faith, even if it is a small amount of faith. God will then nurture that faith and cause it to grow and mature. Even as a gift of faith, faith needs to continue to grow.

God strengthens our faith by allowing us to be placed in circumstances beyond our control. Pastor Dan Keeton gave a devotional regarding that familiar saying that God will not give us more than we can handle. Keeton points out that the Bible does not say that at all. It says, " . . . **will not allow you to be tempted beyond what you are able** . . ." (1 Corinthians 10:13, NASB)

This verse clarifies that God will not allow us to be *tempted* beyond we can handle. In other words, we can't say that we had to give in to sin because there was no other way. God always provides a way out. However, God will allow us to be in situations beyond our abilities. First, He wants us to trust Him and that requires us to be aware that our abilities are limited, but His are unlimited. When things are beyond our control, they are not beyond Him. We can trust in Him always. Second, we must seek God's will in our lives. Placing our faith in Christ also, means to alter our desires and seek the desires He has for us. Third, we must respond to His will. Evangelist Norman Moore provides a great illustration of faith by using the story of Peter walking on water towards Jesus. As we read the story of Jesus walking on the water Peter speaks out to Jesus:

"'Lord, if it is You, command me to come to You on the water.' And He said, 'Come!' And Peter got out of the boat, and walked on the water and came toward Jesus.'" (Matthew 14:28-29, NASB)

Moore says that Peter reacted appropriately in faith. The first response of Peter was to ask if it is the Lord. I can't tell you how many times I have had some good ideas in my life (at least I believe in my mind they are good ideas!). The greatest task I have in being a visionary or "idea guy" is to separate my ideas from the vision that God is giving me.

My ideas may sound worthy, but what I truly want to do is follow the direction of God and do His will. I cannot count how many times I have heard Christians (and sometimes non-Christians) say that God has called them to do a particular task. A popular response I hear is, "God has put this on my heart". I do not doubt that God puts things on our hearts, but first, let's makes sure it is God and not our own thoughts that we claim as God's. Peter first asked, "Lord, if it is you . . ." He is clarifying that the person walking on the water is truly Christ. Satan is well known for trying to lead people out of the will of God. He will also place thoughts in our minds that seem to be great ideas, but the truth is that they are only there to derail us from the plan that God had in our life. Praying to God and confirming that it is God is one of the most critical steps in a walk of faith relationship. You must be sure of two things from the very beginning:

1. "God, is it you?"
2. "If so, then command me."

Peter asked if it was Christ and if it was Christ then, "command me to come to you". This is the foundation building of the walk of faith. The stronger that the foundation can be built the greater the recompense in the walk.

In my walk of faith, I found that God had actually called me when I was very young. However, He did not call me to react to it until I was in my thirties. Confirmation was easy for me in the sense of finding Scripture that calls us to reach the lost, get outside of the mainstream and seek them out. However, I believe we are also to confirm our calling from other Christian leaders or at the least well-grounded Christians. My wife was my first personal confirmation, her lack of hesitation was out of character for her and it showed a great presence of God. God had already enlightened her with the ability to see this was of Him. Dr. Doane was my second personal confirmation, he had no reason to trust such a great outreach to a young computer guy that, as of yet, had not become fully ordained in the Church of the Nazarene. I don't know any other District Superintendent that would have opened the opportunity so easily. Clearly God called Dr. Doane for this occasion! Through these and many others, God was establishing the foundation of the calling. Throughout the next few years I would become so frustrated and overwhelmed that I would continually ask God "Are you in this?" Fortunately, God revealed Himself from the very beginning and I could always look back and see how God had confirmed it many times over and over again. For the purpose of maturing in faith, God continually revealed to me that He was still with me.

One of Satan's strongholds is the ability to bring us down mentally. He normally attacks us when things seem to be out of control. He launches in with many accusations and stirs up plenty of doubt in our abilities and our mission. Your knowledge of this is another critical point in faith—be prepared! Get grounded in your mission and faith, but be prepared to be attacked by the evil one himself. Jesus provides the reaction to these attacks as He was also attacked in the wilderness. "Then Jesus was led up by the Spirit into the wilderness to be tempted by the devil. And after He had fasted forty days and forty nights, He then became hungry. And the tempter came and said to Him, **"If You are the Son of God, command that these stones become bread.' But He answered and said, 'It is written, 'Man shall not live on bread alone, but every word that proceeds out of the mouth of God.'"** (Matthew 4:1-4, NASB)

Satan attacked Christ with doubt. If you are really the Son of God then you should be able to make bread out of the stones. Satan uses Scripture (Psalms 91:11-12) to try and mislead Christ, "**. . . for it is written, 'He will command His angels concerning You; and on their hand they will bear you up, so that you will not strike your foot against a stone.'**" (Matthew 4:6, NASB)

Jesus in both instances quotes Scripture back to Satan (Deuteronomy 6:13, 16 and 10:20). It has always intrigued me that Satan actually uses Scripture to tempt Jesus. But then again, that is similar to what happens often in our own lives. Far too often, I have had the painful experience of hearing of people who have made disastrous decisions because of their misunderstanding of the Scriptures. Satan obviously would love for us to hear his interpretation rather than that of the Holy Spirit. Jesus used the Scripture to defeat the attacks of Satan and we are to use this as an example and do the same. The mission of Christ would have been defeated had Christ given into the temptations. The calling that God gives to each of us can also be destroyed if we are swayed by the tricks of the evil one. The greatest defense is to confirm our calling and get a stronghold on the Word of God. Not merely a reading of the Scripture, but ask the Holy Spirit to give you the meaning of what is being read.

Prayer

Besides a reading of God's Word, Jesus also instructs us that prayer is equally important in our walk of faith.

"Get up and pray that you may not enter into temptation" (Luke 22:46, NASB)

It is also important to pray for each other: "**. . . but I have prayed for you, that your faith may not fail; and you, when once you have turned again, strengthen your brothers.**" (Luke 22:32, NASB)

The tools for a successful walk of faith are at our fingertips, but we must put them to work within our lives. As the trials and tribulations begin to occur, dependency upon God and His Word becomes acute. God expects us to depend upon Him during this process. He wants to build a trusting relationship that is indisputable. As I mentioned earlier, God would place upon my heart to get up out of bed and go get my Bible to read it. It is not by coincidence that He had me open to the words He wanted me to read. It was truly the answer to my prayer. I was raised in a Christian home, so I always read my Bible and prayed. Nevertheless, it wasn't until this experience that I truly found that I not only needed to read and pray as a ritual, but that I literally had to depend upon this process of communicating with God to strengthen and direct me in this walk of faith with Him.

In the illustration of Peter, he first asked Jesus if it was Him. Then, he asked to be commanded, given instruction. And the greatest part of all—Peter obeys. Peter realizes that it is Jesus walking on the water, waits for Him to give the command and then Peter obeys by getting out of the boat. Peter could have put some rational thought into what he was about to do and realize that it is in fact, impossible to walk on water, but he doesn't. He put his faith in the One who commanded him rather than in human intelligence and reason. When God calls us to the ministry, He will also equip us for the ministry, even if the commission does not seem humanly possible. I can't even imagine how shocked Peter must have been when he first realized that he was walking on water, but at some point he must have been in complete awe as he realized what was taking place. As we obey Christ and do His will, we will see some amazing results. Events will take place that are sometimes incomprehensible. In my walk of faith, I was totally surprised that both my wife and Dr. Doane agreed to the project. God had done what seemed impossible in my eyes. God will make a path for us to follow as we seek His will.

As Peter was walking on water towards Christ, the awe turned into fear and he began to notice his surroundings more than his Savior. Peter began to take his attention off of Christ and he began to look at all the activities around him. He began to think of all the fearful things that could happen to him. The waves were stirring up, the winds were blowing and as he took his attention off of Christ, he began to sink: **"But seeing the wind, he became frightened, and beginning to sink, he cried out, "Lord, save me!" Immediately Jesus stretched out His hand and took hold of him, and said to him, 'You of little faith, why did you doubt?'"** (Matthew 14:30-31, NASB)

Evangelist Norman Moore reveals a great insight to this occurrence as he describes that Peter was very close to Christ before he cried out to Him because the Scripture doesn't say that Jesus walked over to Peter or made any movement towards Peter at all—Christ simply stretched out his hand and took hold of him. Peter was only an arm's length away from Christ before the fear set in and faith subsided.

As we mature in our faith the trials and tribulations will continue because of the strengthening process. As a body builder lifts weights to build muscle, heavier weights must be continually added on to continue the process of building muscle. Faith, to be increased, must be exercised at greater levels to increase its ability. Peter got out of the boat and everything seemed to be a great joy. He could see Christ walking on the water and the call to come to Him was fresh in his mind. As Peter began to walk away from the boat and closer to Christ the winds became more apparent to Peter. He is probably too far from the boat to get back in and he can't comprehend his distance to Christ because he is focused on the wind and waves.

There were many times that I became fearful of all the events around me, I was continuously praying to God about losing my home in foreclosure, my daughters' lead poisoning, the $20,000 dental expenses, the financial issues with the concert and the list goes on. I understand Peter's doubt, because that is our human nature and it is also the part that Christ wants to bring us through so that we may have complete assurance of His will and His abilities. He can and will take care of us, we simply need to know this within ourselves. I am the first to acknowledge that I was not the perfect person for taking on such a ministry that God called me to do, but what I have found in my walk is that Christ doesn't look for the most qualified or the most accomplished. God looks for people that will have faith and get out of the boat like Peter. There were eleven other disciples in the boat, but only crazy Peter got out and walked to Christ. There are only two people recorded in the Bible that have ever walked on water; Jesus and Peter. The other disciples could have experienced that miraculous ability but they stayed inside the boat and watched Peter. Christ took Peter by the hand and said, "You of little faith, why did you doubt?" However, little faith that Peter had, the disciples in the boat had "no faith". I would rather hear Christ say, "You of little faith" than to say, "You of no faith". Peter's little faith enabled him to successfully walk on water.

I failed so many times as we strove to put together the 7-7-7 event. But God never failed and that is why He doesn't need people who are completely capable of doing what He is calling us to do; God doesn't need our help—He is God. God develops our faith in Him by asking us to do things that are greater than our abilities and we get to experience first-hand His abilities to accomplish what we are incapable of achieving. Peter wasn't capable of walking on water, but Christ called him to do just that. It wasn't meant to show the strength and abilities of Peter; it was meant to show the strength and abilities of Christ.

Faith—Not so Understood

When Peter got out of the boat, you can imagine what the disciples in the boat may have been thinking. I know from my own experiences that I was considered foolish and unequipped for the task. If the disciples were anything like the people I encountered in my walk, then they were jealous as Peter walked on the water with Jesus and critical as Peter began to sink. For the most part, I realized that our motivation cannot be swayed by public opinion. We should not be swayed to act upon something because people are in agreement and we shouldn't be swayed away because people are in disagreement—we must act upon Christ's calling and leading to do His will; no matter what people say nor how they react.

One of the issues of walking by faith is the "not knowing". There are so many times that people would ask me questions like, "How are we going to do that?", "How can we afford that?", "What do we do next?" and "When is the money coming in?" As I mentioned earlier, God uses His Word to lead us and this is why it is so important to read it continually. The questions began to overtake me mentally because I did not actually have the answers. To walk by faith is not seeing what you hope for, **"Now faith is the assurance of things hoped for, the conviction of things not seen."** (Hebrews 11:1-3, NASB)

It was impossible for me to answer because I did not have the answer. Then, I remembered the story of Moses and I read through it over and over again as I walked in faith. Moses was continually dealing with people that were questioning the mission where they were headed and how they would get there.

"Then they said to Moses, 'Is it because there were no graves in Egypt that you have taken us away to die in the wilderness? Why have you dealt with us in this way, bringing us out of Egypt? Is this not the word that we spoke to you in Egypt, saying, 'Leave us alone that we may serve the Egyptians'? For it would have been better for us to serve the Egyptians than to die in the wilderness.'" (Exodus 14:11-12, NASB)

Moses did not have a clue. He continuously had to ask God and wait for God to reveal the answers. Most people do not understand faith and will turn from a mission that is faith driven. It is a difficult task to walk by faith and hope for things that you cannot see; but, it is an even greater task to lead others in a walk of faith in things that neither you nor they can see. In this world, it takes money to accomplish big goals; but, with God it takes faith. For a ministry to walk by faith, the people must all agree to walk by faith. The families must agree to walk by faith or the enemy will use the family to weaken the motivation. Many times Jesus was criticized and mocked for His faith. At one point a little girl was dead and people were mourning her death. When He said that she was not dead but just sleeping, they all began to laugh. We are not to expect people to understand our walk of faith, but we are to act upon our faith and let God do the rest. Who was laughing when the girl got up?

"He said, 'Leave; for the girl has not died, but is asleep.' And they began laughing at Him. But when the crowd had been sent out, He entered and took her by the hand, and the girl got up. This news spread throughout all that land." (Matthew 9:24-26, NASB)

Share the Experience

There were times where I noticed that my wife and I were not at the same point in our faith. Just as I had to include my wife in my prayer life, I also needed to include her in my walk of faith. It was largely due to me trying to handle all the issues alone. I did not want to overburden my wife with the financial and contractual issues. This became a detrimental mistake on my behalf. God did not expect me to take on the burden alone. He is not looking for any of us to be the Lone Ranger; instead, He is building a body of believers. After I realized that I had been growing in faith because I was able to see first-hand how God was walking us through amazing challenges, I then realized that my wife was not seeing the evidence because I had been secluding her from it, thinking I was protecting her from the issues. One interesting point of the Bible is that it doesn't only speak of all the positive things, but it also includes the failures. The life of David does not only reveal his obedience to God, but also the disobedience; the wisdom and wealth of Solomon, and also the fickleness and spoils of Solomon; the failures of the disciples (especially Judas) and the continual faithlessness of the Jewish people. God does not hide the issues of this world while He is revealing His miraculous abilities to overcome this world's misfortunes. As we walk through the life of faith we are to share the walk with our brothers and sisters in Christ, so that they may also see the hand of God work within them. My wife's faith began to grow with my faith as I began to share the tribulations with her. Then, we would be more open to the others within the ministry and they also would begin to grow stronger in the faith. People began to pray more diligently for the each other and the ministry. Faith is to be shared. It is often misunderstood and sometimes considered "stupidity", but as God reveals His miraculous work, the foolishness is eliminated and faith remains.

God's Not Too Busy

The previous Bible story of the little girl being brought to life is a great illustration of faith and waiting upon God. The girl's father had come to Christ and asked Him to come and save his daughter who had died. Jesus began to follow him when Jesus suddenly stopped. He turned around and was looking for the person who had just touched Him.

"While He was saying these things to them, a synagogue official came and bowed down before Him, and said, 'My daughter has just died; but come and lay Your hand on her, and she will live.' Jesus got up and began to follow him, and so did His disciples. And a woman who had been suffering from a hemorrhage for twelve years, came up behind Him and touched the fringe of His cloak; for she was saying to herself, 'If I only touch His garment, I will get well.' But Jesus turning and seeing her said, 'Daughter, take courage; your faith has made you well.' At once the woman was made well." (Matthew 9:18-22, NASB) *See Mark 5:25-42 for additional details.*

I often wonder what the father of the little girl must have been thinking. His daughter is dying and Jesus is looking for someone who touched His clothes. I think I would be a very frustrated dad at this point. However, there is a message here that Jesus is never too late nor ever too busy. Jesus stopped and helped a woman that had touched Him in faith. She had been sick for twelve years and she had faith to know that if she could just touch the clothes of Jesus she would be healed. Jesus stopped to acknowledge this woman of faith; he wasn't looking to scold her, rather, to uplift her. There are many times that we see other Christians being blessed as we are going through tribulations. It is a hard moment in our life, but we are to have faith that our moment is coming and that we also will experience the miracle that Christ has for us. The girl's dad must have been a bit surprised, frustrated and anxious as Christ was healing this woman; yet, not long afterwards, Christ continued the journey to his home and raised the girl to life. As we walk by faith, we are learning to place our entire life in the control of God's will and not our own. This means that we accept the outcome of God's will.

I often teach about the story of Jesus raising Lazarus from the dead. The story begins with Christ being sent a message that His friend Lazarus was deathly sick. Jesus did not get up quickly and go to see Lazarus, but rather He waited for a day or so and then began the journey to see him. Jesus commented to His disciples that Lazarus was dead and that He was going to raise him from the dead. As Jesus reached the tomb, He wept. Many people believe that Jesus felt so sad for Lazarus that He was weeping. I want to be clear and state that I am not a Theologian; however, this thought does not make sense to me. Why would Jesus be sad if He knew that He was going to bring Lazarus back to life in a matter of seconds? I see it as Christ knows what is on the other side of death for those that love Him. I deeply believe that Christ knew that Lazarus had the opportunity to be in Paradise, but for the Glory of God to be revealed to others, He would raise Lazarus from the dead (bring him from a wonderful perfect place) back to this painful sinful world. My mother died a few years ago and many people questioned why God did not answer our prayers and heal her from Alzheimer's and diabetes. I love my mom and miss her, but would I want her to be back in this world compared to the one she is in now? Not a chance. God did answer our prayers, Betty Jeanne Karanick is in Heaven with the Almighty God, talking to Jesus Himself and having a pain free eternal life! She is no longer legally blind, no Alzheimer's, no diabetes, and no more doctor visits. As we walk by faith, we begin to understand that God knows what is best for us; here and in eternity.

After the 7-7-7 Concert at the Rose Bowl Stadium, I did get a call to speak at youth camp for the Los Angeles District Church of the Nazarene. I remember spending the week and had a fairly decent response to people accepting Christ. However, there were some gang members who were also attending camp. They basically kept to themselves except for staring me down every once in a while. I believe that one of the gang members was a preacher's kid and that is why they were attending. The girls that spent a lot of time with them had mentioned to me that they (the girls) had been thinking of accepting Christ at the invitations, but they just hadn't done it. On the final night of camp, no one responded to the altar call. It wasn't discouraging because they had been responding all week. I almost closed the final service and then I remembered that the girls had told me that they had almost come down each night. So, I gave everyone a final invitation and once again—no one. I began to pray and close the service when someone slid a chair across the floor. It was so loud that I looked up and one of the gang members began to walk down to me. He stood directly in front of me and said, "It is me. You have been waiting on me. I want to get saved." After that, nearly the entire youth camp came down and prayed.

After about an hour of praying with everyone, someone tapped me on the shoulder. They pointed to one of the gang members and said, "He wants to talk to you." I didn't know what to think, but I began to approach him and he was shaking tremendously and staring me directly in my eyes. He muttered something about a flag. I said, "I'm sorry but I don't understand what you said." He was shaking so much that his voice was distorted and he muttered again, "I dropped my flag." I responded, "I'm sorry, I don't know what that means." I dropped my flag, my bandana that hides my face. I accepted Christ tonight and I quit gang banging. They will probably hunt me down, but I quit." God had changed some serious lives and I got to witness it. This reconfirmed that God wasn't done with the ministry just yet.

I returned home and as before, we were completely broke and we began our life again with almost nothing to our name. God continued to take care of us and I began to place my resume online to take on a job of any kind. I have driven a bus for the church for many years so; I decided to send my resume to agencies that hire truck drivers. No one called—no one! I have a family and I need to provide a place to live and food for them all. I must have asked God many times, "Why can't you just help me get a job?" This seems like such a small task for such a powerful God. A few more days of stressing out went by when I received a call from a job recruiter. It was about 4:00 pm and she asked me typical employment questions and then asked, "Can you start tomorrow at 4:30 in the morning?" In total amazement and a bit scared that I am going to work in less than 12 hours, I replied, "Sure". I began driving a truck to construction sites delivering plumbing supplies. The first week on the job, I was sent out with another driver as part of the training process. As soon as we entered the truck, the driver began telling me all about the company, his life and the things to look out for. During the conversation, he literally incorporated a cuss word into every other word or so (he cussed a lot). We pulled over to get some coffee and as we pulled into the parking area, he asked, "Where did you work before coming here?" "Oh, I am a preacher", I said. He quickly responded, "That is awesome. I am a Christian too." He continued to cuss as we went throughout the day, but every so often he would catch himself and apologize. It did not offend me, I just found it interesting. Eventually, I was the driver and they would have a helper go along with me to make deliveries. Being the driver, I chose the radio station to listen to while on the road. I always listened to my very favorite Air1 Christian music station or Calvary Chapel's KWAVE, a Christian Bible teaching station. I always had a backpack with me and I kept a few giveaway Bibles in it. Each time I had a new helper, I would give him a Bible. It wasn't long until I was no longer called Paul; they called me Preacher. I found it interesting that more and more the guys would start to ask me questions about the Bible. It was as if God placed me in a truck with people for 8 hours a day to talk to them about His Word. One day, I had to be the helper and not the driver because they needed me to help one of the drivers on his route. I knew this driver but not very well; but, he knew that I was the preacher and I talked about Jesus and listened to Christian radio. Now, I am in his truck and all the drivers are watching him take the wheel. He laughs at the others and says, "We are on the highway to hell today." He instantly turns the music up (not a Christian station) and is having a great party in a sense. I love to listen to Christian music, but I know that this is his truck and his rules. I am OK with that. We get on the road and not ten minutes later he turns the music down and for the next 7 or so hours, as he was weeping, he had told me his whole life story. He was looking for answers, but was having a hard time accepting them. I heard about his "wife" (whom he is not married to officially), his girlfriend (who is the one he says he loves and carries a picture of her in the truck) and his son who had almost died in a severe accident. Throughout the day, I realized he was seeking a Savior but was not willing to give his life to Him yet. I gave him a Bible. He said, "I will take it and maybe one day when I am sitting at home on the couch, who knows, I may read it." Later that week, his buddy ended up being my helper as I drove the truck. I gave him a Bible and he didn't say much of anything about it. I began to witness at every construction site and started questioning if Christ had taken me from the concert ministry to place me in the truck driver ministry. I loved it no matter what the case, but I sure was interested in knowing what God was doing.

I got a call late one night from one of the drivers. His world was in such turmoil that he was going to take his own life. After talking with him for a while, he finally said that he would call me back. I was trying to get his address and other information but he kept avoiding it. He finally hangs up and I just knew that I had no way to rescue him. About ten minutes later which seemed like an eternity, he called me back. He said that as we were talking he knew that he was doing the wrong thing, so he hung up the phone, ran to his neighbor's house and asked them to carry him to the hospital. They were leaving as he returned my call.

After a few months, one of the helpers stopped me in the warehouse while I was unloading my truck and he said, "I opened that book you gave me and started reading it. I don't understand a lot about it. Like, what do the two little dots mean?" I asked, "Two dots?" He said, "When I wanted to look up "hope" it had a name, a number, and two dots, then more numbers." I asked, "You mean something like John 3:16?" Sometimes we church folk take for granted the terms and symbols we use. I definitely did. As we reach the lost with the Gospel of Jesus Christ we must realize that many people have never opened a Bible. Do not be afraid to point out and highlight Scriptures that will be helpful for someone seeking Christ.

Xclaimed Ministries was now a small group of people who would meet every Saturday night for Praise and Worship. It was just a handful of people (less than ten) but then it began to increase to about 25 or so. At this point I really had not figured out what God was calling my wife and me to do. Where is our ministry now that the concert is complete?

When I went to work one morning, my route had been changed. They needed me to drive out about four hours or so to deliver some items to another branch. As I got on the road, I began to pray and just ask God what he intended for my life. Financially we had not recovered so bills were adding up, and the ministry was not growing as we would like, and I was always exhausted after driving a truck all day. I asked God over and over, "Are you in this? If you are in this then I am OK with whatever you have planned, but I need to know that you are with me!" I prayed like this for over an hour as I was driving along and felt at peace with what I had discussed with God. I laid everything out to Him and left it in His hands. I turned on the radio to a Christian station out in nowhere land and sure enough the sermon was just beginning and was titled, "I Will Never Leave You". I could not stop rejoicing in the fact that God had perfect timing and to me that was the answer I needed to hear. On the return trip, another pastor was on the radio and his message was on the same topic and he was emphasizing that God is with us. Later that evening, as I was driving home, another pastor had a very similar message. These sermons could have been on any topic that day, but God heard me cry out and He answered. I was familiar with these Bible verses that the pastors were teaching on, but God brought them to life as I needed them.

Looking Forward in Faith

Weeks later, I began to think of how our ministry could do concerts again. I still believe that the church needs to get into the community and reach the people. If a man is drowning, he doesn't swim to the lifeguard, the lifeguard swims out to him. The church should not expect the lost to find their way to Jesus; the church needs to bring Jesus to the lost. The more I thought about the concerts, I realized that we needed a stage. Every day I drove to construction sites, but on one of those days, God showed me exactly what I needed to look for. All these sites use scaffolding! I began to draw up ideas for building a stage out of scaffolding. I began to call different companies that sold scaffolding and they provided ideas that could accomplish what I was envisioning. Finally, I had it all put together and it was too expensive for us. That seemed to knock the wind right out of me. I really thought we were headed somewhere with this stage idea. I simply turned it over to God and left it at that. As I made a stop one day at one of the construction sites, I was talking with one of the foremen about my plan. In less than a heartbeat, he said, "Here is the number of a company to call. They have great prices." Sure enough, it was half the price of anyone else. In fact, when I called the other companies to see if they could match the price (I felt I owed them at least the opportunity since they had helped me along so far) they said that it was impossible for that company to give us the scaffolding for that low. That confirmed we had a great price and we could afford it. We now owned a self-designed stage and was hoping it would work!

I guess the next question was, "What were we going to do with the stage?" After a few weeks, I was talking with Dave Cadena, the former Mayor of Stanton, and he offered to help. He called some people in the Park and Recreations Department of the City of Stanton and got us the approval to use Stanton Park for one Saturday. Gary McGinnis from Placentia Grace Community Church said he would let us use his sound equipment. We started making fliers to advertise the next concert event and the church attendance began to pick up. I had envisioned everything being free for the community and that we would provide food for everyone, free toys for every child in attendance and free bicycles for a few of the children (We would draw names for those). The concert began and approximately 450 people attended. Everyone received a free cheeseburger meal grilled on our eight gas burner BBQ grill, every child received a free toy and we gave away ten new bicycles. The band played, I delivered a message of Hope through Jesus Christ and about 8% of the people came down to accept Christ into their life.

God had now provided the answer to the direction for the ministry. My wife and I originally walked by faith to produce a concert at the Rose Bowl Stadium. We believe that this concert was the end to what God had called us to do. I personally thought that if others saw what a small group of people could do to outreach, imagine how much more would be possible if many began to outreach. Now, I see that that was not exactly what God intended for our walk with Him. We began to average between 50 to 60 people at our Saturday night worship and almost half of them were children. We began to work closely with the City of Stanton as they realized that we were actively helping the people within the city. We were later approved to have 'Concerts in the Park' every other month. The concerts averaged 300-350 people and consistently had an 8-10% response to the opportunity to accept Christ.

It did not take long before we truly understood that Christ was using us in this outreach to the community and based on percentages we were accomplishing close to the same responses as the larger evangelistic events.

Although we could see a bit of where God was leading us, we still had no idea where we would actually end up. The 'Concert in the Park' which we named "REVIVE!" became the one most important thing that we had to do and we looked forward to getting it accomplished. It wasn't long before we tried to improve our outreach ministry to include an amusement carnival with all the rides and booths. Over a three day period we had ministered to thousands of people and had given away many bicycles and Bibles.

I remember the last day, the finale, I had an altar call and many people came forward. I noticed that one of the carnival workers came down also. Later that night, I was leaving the park and I saw that same carnival worker at the very first booth near the front entrance. I waved and said, "It was good to see you come down for prayer." She replied, "I was listening to you during your message, but I had to stay here at the booth (about 100 yards from the stage). However, when you asked if anyone would like to accept Christ in their life, I looked at my boss and told him I had to go down to the stage. He said, 'You can't leave your booth.' I said, Watch me. I left my booth and ran down to accept Christ as you prayed with everyone. I prayed, too!" She continued to tell me why she knew she needed Jesus in her life. As we finished talking, I began to walk away and I saw the man that was in charge of the carnival crew. He stopped me and said, "I heard what you said up on the stage. You mentioned that anyone who would like a Bible could have one. Can I get one?" I gave him a Bible and a Book of John. The following morning when we were completing the tear down of the event, he saw me and said, "I read the Book of John last night. Maybe I'll start going to church one of these days."

Blessed with Bibles

At each event we were determined to give a Bible to every person in attendance. We know that if the Word of God reaches the homes of the people their lives will change. It may be a while before anyone actually opens it up to read, but we feel confident that it will be read. The Lockman Foundation was told about our outreach and determined that they would like to provide the Bibles needed at each event. God knew that we could not afford to keep purchasing Bibles, but He knew a group that had the same desire to spread the Gospel into every home and HE connected them to us. I can't put into words the amount of appreciation I have for the Lockman Foundation to choose such a small group like ours and keep us stocked with the tools necessary to distribute Bibles at each event.

"Concert in the Park"

Eventually, we made a decision to try to have the 'REVIVE!' events at our own church on the half acre behind the building. This would give people the opportunity to see where we are located and also give us more time to set up the stage a day prior to the event. The major issue was being so close to the neighbors. The City gave us a permit to have the event and we decided to be extra neighbor conscious. Days before the event we sent out a notice to the neighbors and one day before the event, we took chocolate chip cookies to all the closest neighbors. When the day of the concert began the Sheriff arrived. One of the neighbors (only one) had called and complained. It is the same neighbor that uses our park every day to walk his dog without permission.

I took the permit to the Sheriff and said, "This is our permit, but if you say we should stop we will take it all down right away." He said, "You have a permit that says the City has given you approval. Plus, you are helping the community. Why would I ask you to stop that?"

Xclaimed Team and Bicycle Winners at "Concert in the Park"

The event worked out so well that we began to do all our events at our own location. From March to September, every other month, we would have a concert in the back of our church. We gave away a lot of chocolate chip cookies to the neighbors and they began to ask for extras. Some of the neighborhood kids would come over and participate in the activities (two of them won bicycles at one of the events). In addition, we started a Christmas Festival which would be held inside the church. The first year we had just around 300 people; the next year, over 500 people and the third year over 1,080 people. As a result of our community outreach events, we began to meet many of the people in the community and hear the individual stories of their own lives. Many of them lived in the local motels, and are considered homeless due to the fact that a motel is not a permanent residence. These families live in a small motel room and many have children, one or more grandparents and other extended family also living in the same room. It did not take long to realize that God was sending us to assist these families. The Cities of Stanton and Anaheim have a great amount of people who live in the motels. There are drugs, prostitution, child molesters and many other filthy lifestyles living in these motels as well. It is truly no place for a child. As a church, we would like to help everyone who needs help. God gave me the insight to realize that we are not called to help everyone. Some are called in different areas of ministry and it is important to seek the calling that God has given. We could see that we were not equipped to assist people on drugs, alcohol, or other addictions. However, we found that we have a real gift to offer a safe place for children. We began to pick the children up at the motels and apartments to bring them to church. The parents wanted a break from the kids and the kids probably wanted to get away from the parents and tons of others living in their motel room. As the children began to come to church, they would want to stay at church. Many would call daily to see if we were having anything at the church.

We began seeing these same kids at school where our kids attend school. There was one kid in my daughter's class that wanted nothing to do with church. My daughter (1st grade), would always ask him to come, but he would always say no. One day, I think it was family fun night or movie night, he decided he wanted to come to church. From that day on, he would always ask if he could come to church. I went to the motel to pick him up and his mother and sister (age 4) walked him to the bus. The four year old girl flipped us off and said a few cuss words. People all around thought it was funny and began to laugh. This happened several other times. I finally had enough. I took it to the church that night and said tonight we are going to pray for this little girl. She is living in an environment where people think this type of behavior is cute. We as a church can pray this week for change in her life. The brother (age 6) was one of the first to come to the altar to pray for his sister. The next time I went to the motel to pick him up I did not have as many people to pick up so I took our old 1985 Dodge 15 passenger van. I opened the door for the boy and he jumped in and closed the door. I was in a hurry for some reason, but about two miles later I looked in the rearview mirror and realized that the little girl had also gotten in the van to come to church with her brother. I smiled and thought to myself, how powerful is prayer! She came to church and God changed her life. They both continue to come to church regularly.

God used these two children to help us move into our next phase of God's purpose. The mom of the two children could not stay in the motel any longer. She had a place to stay but could not keep the kids with her. Needless to say, since we had an extra bedroom in our home the two moved in with us for a few days, which became a few weeks, then over a year. During their stay, two other motel kids began coming to church who also attended the same school. One day, I noticed they were no longer coming to church or to school. I called their mom and she said that they had changed motels and it was too far to bring the kids to school or church. I offered to pick them up early in the morning to get them to school each day. After a few weeks, it became a bit expensive with gas prices reaching $4.00 a gallon to keep driving so far. My wife and I offered to let them stay at our home with all the other kids. The motel they were currently staying at had one room and many adults living in the room. The mom was thrilled with the idea and they stayed a little over three months. Their mom eventually got a different place to live and they all moved back in together. Almost a week after they were situated, a lady that noticed all the kids staying at our home began to talk to my wife. She said that she and her daughters just lost their place to stay and are basically on the streets. Normally, we would not allow other adults to live in our home, but in this case, since we knew them from the school, we made an exception with strict guidelines and a specific time limit. Months later they were able to move into a place of their own. Other families from the church asked if their children could stay with us during hardships, which we would generally allow for short terms.

Our ministry had reached into the community and found that we not only provided food, toys, Bibles and the message of Jesus Christ, but we were reaching the children and their lives were changing. They first two children that stayed with us began to change their language as they also improved in their school work. The teachers were amazed by how they had changed and even began to receive awards because of their accomplishments. Our ministry cannot change everyone, but we can provide help to the families that need help within our community. It seems that we are constantly seeing the direction that God is leading us and it appears to be growing rapidly. We have quickly moved from being primarily a concert outreach to an outreach centered around helping children and low income families.

Children Chasing Bubbles at "Concert in the Park"

In the midst of all the amazing work God was doing, He was also opening doors for the ministry. The Xclaimed Band consisted of members from Anaheim Calvary Chapel, Chino Hills Calvary Chapel, and the Cerritos Crossroads Multinational Church of the Nazarene. As I mentioned earlier, the sound equipment is from a member of the Placentia Grace Church. Many of the volunteers that help cook and serve the food come from La Palma Christian Center, Whittier College Avenue Church and Sea Coast Grace. The Church of the Nazarene recognized us as a Compassionate Ministry Center and over 20 news articles have been published by news agencies such as OCNEWS, Christian Examiner, NCN NEWS, Orange County Register, Yahoo News, and many other online news agencies as well.

Toy line at "Concert in the Park"

My wife and I had housed over twelve children in our home in a matter of a year or so. It was obvious that we could not house every needy child, but God definitely let us know which ones we could help. I received a call just before Christmas by an Administrator with Social Services. He said, "Pastor Paul, I have four children that say that they can stay with you." Without going into details, they had been separated from their family and when they were asked by Social Services if they knew any close family they could stay with, they said, "Pastor Paul and Pastor Tina will let us stay with them". Yes, they were correct. They had actually stayed with us for a few months in the past and that is why they were so sure of having a place to stay with us now. Just before Christmas, all four of them became our official foster children. Had they not been able to stay with us the other option was that they would be separated into different foster homes and we couldn't see that happening.

During our process of taking in so many children, Norman Moore, of Norman Moore Ministries, felt the need to help us purchase a van to shuttle all these children from place to place. He wanted to do a bit of fundraising within the local churches and see what he could raise.

After a few days, he talked it over with his wife, Vickie, and she responded, "Why don't you do it? That's what Jesus told his disciples to do." Norman Moore drove to the church, picked me up and took me to an auto dealer and purchased us a well-running used Ford van. It was a miracle that only God could have done and only from people as dedicated to listening to God as Norman and Vickie. The illustration that Vickie used came from the story of Jesus feeding the five thousand.

"But the crowds were aware of this and followed Him; and welcoming them, He began speaking to them about the kingdom of God and curing those who had need of healing. Now the day was ending, and the twelve came and said to Him, 'Send the crowd away, that they may go into the surrounding villages and countryside and find lodging and get something to eat; for here we are in a desolate place.' But He said to them, 'You give them something to eat!' And they said, 'We have no more than five loaves and two fish, unless perhaps we go and buy food for all these people.'" (Luke 9:11-15, NASB)

We are the Body of Christ

As we grow in our faith, others will begin to depend upon our faith. We as the body of Christ must work together in faith. It is one thing to see a need within people, but it is by the work of faith that we become the body of Christ as we respond to the need. I do not believe that every home should be opened up to helping house children in need. It is a bit risky and it is not a calling for every Christian. However, it is a calling for us to put our faith to work. We are to be the arms, eyes and ears of Christ. He desires to do His work through us. He told his disciples to go out and heal the sick and raise the dead. Sure, Jesus could just do it Himself, but he wants a relationship with us. As a father, I can install the new digital television on my own. I do not need anyone's help to do so. My son, on the other hand, needs to feel as if he is part of my life. As he stands and watches me with the screws and wires, he is in total amazement with all the things going on. But, when I ask him to help me—he becomes part of the amazement. God doesn't need us to do His work; we are the ones that need it. Through our involvement we feel and connect to God's abilities and it completely amazes us. Not only do we, as a church body, feel the work of God, but others around us see it happening. They become witnesses to His work through us. People are looking to see Christ and we are that connection that they have. They can see Christ through us. When the disciples approached Jesus and said to send the people away so that they could get food, He responded that they (the disciples) should feed them. As we grow in our faith from a small seed to an enormous tree, we look to getting to the place that we realize God will provide. The disciples at this point could only see how little they had, but Jesus wanted them to see, through Him, how much they had. Jesus wants us to be confident that He will supply. We bring the multitude to Him and He will provide the necessities. It is worth noting that Jesus provided by giving to His disciples and they gave to the people. God expects us to work our faith. As we grow in our faith, God expects us to use it. The verse of the mustard seed says that the seed grows into a tree that the birds can nest in. It is through the faith of the church body in the power of Jesus Christ that others will witness His amazing power and Grace.

There are many times that we seem to be inadequate for the calling that God has placed upon us. My wife and I, by far, were inadequately qualified for the task that God had placed upon us. As we struggled with each aspect of growing in faith, we came to realize the most important points of having faith; to primarily be sure that the calling is of God. Building that strong foundation of confirmation will prove vital in the developing process. Second, by understanding that God doesn't need the qualified; He needs the willing. God will provide all of our needs for the ministry He has called us to do. God is faithful and will provide until the work is complete.

Conclusion

Jesus wants us to grow in our faith. Some, or probably most of us, start out fearful and with only a small amount of faith. I do not believe it is coincidence that Jesus used the mustard seed as the example in His parable on faith. He used the smallest seed to show that through growth we can all mature into enormous amounts of faith that will be a testimony to many others struggling in their faith.

After the ministry began, I looked back on how God had walked us through the ministry and taught us how to rely on Him; I realized that God had specifically taken time to reveal His power and ability years before we ever started the ministry. About 2004, my wife, daughter and I went to Hawaii with her family. My wife couldn't wait to get everyone together to tell the exciting news that she is pregnant. At the very beginning of the trip her dad, my daughter and I all ended up getting sick. My wife postponed breaking the news until the final day that we were in Hawaii, which is when we all felt a little less sick. Everyone was so excited to hear the news as we were all on the beach for hours talking about it and planning the future.

Because I had been so sick for most of the trip I hadn't been able to go snorkeling. Feeling somewhat better towards the end of our vacation, I decided it was time to try. My sister-in-law also wanted to go snorkeling and possibly see some turtles. As I mentioned, I had been sick all week and was still fairly weak. After going out a ways, we got caught in a rip tide which pulled us out over one hundred yards from the coast. After a long struggle trying to reach the shore, I was eventually too weak to continue to try. My sister-in-law finally made it to shore and went for help. I was simply too far from the shore and I began to realize that my life was over. I looked around many times for help but there was no one in the water nor anyone on shore paying attention to rescue me. I looked towards my wife and family to take a last glimpse of my daughter and wife, but they were too far away. My leg cramped up, my energy was drained and I was done. I struggled to stay afloat as long as I could, calculating that I could stay afloat at least another 30 seconds or so. God spoke to me as only He can (through the Spirit, not by an audible voice) and asked me to look to my right. I am so frustrated that I angrily responded, "I have looked everywhere, there is nowhere to go." I then obeyed and looked to the right. Sure enough, two surfers were just ten yards away from me. I shouted out for help and one came to my rescue and carried me to shore on his surfboard. He went back into the water and I have never seen him again.

This event took place a year or so before my wife and I committed to or even dreamed of this ministry, but this was God's early teaching to me that I needed to trust Him. Trust Him even when I can't see any hope. This was a prelude to the events that would be taking place over the next few years. I would find plenty of times where I would feel like I was spiritually and physically dying. God would repeatedly prove to me that He exists and that He will always be with me through it all. He allowed me to be alone in the ocean, seconds from death, to reveal that He has no limits on His ability to provide. There is no such thing as "too late" with God. He can rescue us at any point and the sooner we understand the power that He has the sooner we can grow in our faith.

As you walk in Christ, walk by faith and not by sight. There are many times that you will not be able to see how things could be changed, but be confident that God can do anything in His time, His perfect time. He has no limits—none. He will never leave you nor forsake you if you have a relationship with Him.

About the Author

Left to right: Nathan, Paul, Christina, Hannah and Grace

Paul Karanick is an ordained Pastor in the Church of the Nazarene and has a Bachelor of Science Degree in Biblical Studies from Indiana Wesleyan University. However, he will be the first to point out that he learned his greatest Biblical teachings from his mom and dad. He was born a preacher's kid and learned through their faith, to have faith in Christ. Remarkably, Paul did not want to preach. He remembers praying as a teenager, "God, I will do anything that you want me to do, but please don't call me to preach." Years later, not only was Paul called to preach, but he co-founded Xclaimed Ministries with his wife, Christina. Paul claims that in his later years he prayed, "God, I love this! Why didn't you call me sooner?"

Paul's gift of faith is extraordinary and he lives his life by the Scripture "Walk by faith; not by sight" (2 Corinthians 5:7). He enjoys teaching others to walk by faith as well, revealing a closer walk with Christ. Through this same type of faith, Xclaimed Ministries has been able to outreach and provide for needs within the community in a very unique way.

NOTES

Made in the USA
Lexington, KY
18 June 2013